POCKET
BOOKS

ALSO BY MARCUS BUCKINGHAM

First, Break All the Rules
The One Thing You Need to Know

Now, Discover Your Strengths

How to develop your talents and those of the people you manage

**MARCUS BUCKINGHAM &
DONALD O. CLIFTON**

POCKET
BOOKS

LONDON • SYDNEY • NEW YORK • TORONTO

First published in Great Britain by Pocket Books, 2004
This edition published by Pocket Books, 2005
An imprint of Simon & Schuster UK Ltd
A CBS COMPANY

10

Simon & Schuster UK Ltd
Africa House
64–78 Kingsway
London WC2B 6AH

www.simonsays.co.uk

Simon & Schuster Australia
Sydney

A CIP catalogue record for this book is
available from the British Library.

ISBN-13: 978-1-4165-0265-4

Printed and bound in Great Britain by
Cox & Wyman Ltd, Reading, Berkshire

to my wife, Jane, strong enough for three . . .
    —MARCUS

to those who helped me discover my strengths—
my wife, Shirley, and our family
    —DON

Contents

Chapter 6. Managing Strengths

Chapter 7. Building a Strengths-based Organization

Appendix

Introduction:
The Strengths Revolution at Work

Guided by the belief that good is the opposite of bad, mankind has for centuries pursued its fixation with fault and failing. Doctors have studied disease in order to learn about health. Psychologists have investigated sadness in order to learn about joy. Therapists have looked into the causes of divorce in order to learn about happy marriage. And in schools and workplaces around the world, each one of us has been encouraged to identify, analyze, and correct our weaknesses in order to become strong.

This advice is well intended but misguided. Faults and failings deserve study, but they reveal little about strengths. Strengths have their own patterns.

To excel in your chosen field and to find lasting satisfaction in doing so, you will need to understand your unique patterns. You will need to become an expert at finding and describing and applying and practicing and refining your strengths. So as you read this book, shift your focus. Suspend whatever interest you may have in weakness and instead explore the intricate detail of your strengths. Take the StrengthsFinder Profile. Learn its language. Discover the source of your strengths.

If by the end of the book you have developed your expertise in what is *right* about you and your employees, this book will have served its purpose.

The Revolution

"What are the two assumptions on which great organizations must be built?"

We wrote this book to start a revolution, the strengths revolution. At the heart of this revolution is a simple decree: The great organization must not only accommodate the fact that each employee is different, *it must capitalize on these differences*. It must watch for clues to each employee's natural talents and then position and develop each employee so that his or her talents are transformed into bona fide strengths. By changing the way it selects, measures, develops, and channels the careers of its people, this revolutionary organization must build its entire enterprise around the strengths of each person.

And as it does, this revolutionary organization will be positioned to dramatically outperform its peers. In our latest meta-analysis The Gallup Organization asked this question of 198,000 employees working in 7,939 business units within 36 companies: At work do you have the opportunity to do what you do best every day? We then compared the responses to the performance of the business units and discovered the following: When employees answered "strongly agree" to this question, they were 50 percent more likely to work in business units with lower employee turnover, 38 percent more likely to work in more productive business units, and 44 percent more likely to work in business units with higher customer satisfaction scores. And over time those business units that increased the number of employees who strongly agreed saw comparable increases in productivity, customer loyalty, and employee retention. Whichever way you care to slice the data, the organization whose employees feel that their strengths are used every day is more powerful and more robust.

This is very good news for the organization that wants to be on the vanguard of the strengths revolution. Why? Because most organizations remain startlingly inefficient at capitalizing on the strengths of their people. In Gallup's total database we have asked the "opportunity to do what I do best" question of more than 1.7 million employees in 101 companies from 63 countries. What percentage do you think strongly agrees that they have an opportunity to do what they do best every day? What percentage truly feels that their strengths are in play?

Twenty percent. Globally, only 20 percent of employees working in the large organizations we surveyed feel that their strengths are in play every day. Most bizarre of all, the longer an employee stays with an organization and the higher he climbs the traditional career ladder, the less likely he is to strongly agree that he is playing to his strengths.

Alarming though it is to learn that most organizations operate at 20 percent capacity, this discovery actually represents a tremendous opportunity for great organizations. To spur high-margin growth and thereby increase their value, great organizations need only focus inward to find the wealth of unrealized capacity that resides in every single employee. Imagine the increase in productivity and profitability if they doubled this number and so had 40 percent of their employees strongly agreeing that they had a chance to use their strengths every day. Or how about tripling the number? Sixty percent of employees saying "strongly agree" isn't too aggressive a goal for the greatest organizations.

How can they achieve this? Well, to begin with they need to understand why eight out of ten employees feel somewhat miscast in their role. What can explain this widespread inability to position people—in particular senior people who have had the chance to search around for interesting roles—to play to their strengths?

The simplest explanation is that most organizations' basic assumptions about people are wrong. We know this because for the last thirty years Gallup has been conducting research into the best way to maximize a person's potential. At the heart of this research are our interviews with eighty thousand managers—most excellent, some average—in hundreds of organizations around the world. Here the focus was to discover what the world's best managers (whether in Bangalore or Bangor) had in common. We described our discoveries in detail in the book *First, Break All the Rules,* but the most significant finding was this: Most organizations are built on two flawed assumptions about people:

1. Each person can learn to be competent in almost anything.

2. Each person's greatest room for growth is in his or her areas of greatest weakness.

Presented so baldly, these two assumptions seem too simplistic to be commonly held, so let's play them out and see where they lead. If you want to test whether or not your organization is based on these assumptions, look for these characteristics:

- Your organization spends more money on training people once they are hired than on selecting them properly in the first place.

- Your organization focuses the performance of its employees by legislating work style. This means a heavy emphasis on work rules, policies, procedures, and "behavioral competencies."

- Your organization spends most of its training time and money on trying to plug the gaps in employees' skills or competencies. It calls these gaps "areas of opportunity." Your individual development plan, if you have one, is built around your "areas of opportunity," your weaknesses.

- Your organization promotes people based on the skills or experiences they have acquired. After all, if everyone can learn to be competent in almost anything, those who have learned the most must be the most valuable. Thus, by design, your organization gives the most prestige, the most respect, and the highest salaries to the most experienced well-rounded people.

Finding an organization that doesn't have these characteristics is more difficult than finding one that does. Most organizations take their employees' strengths for granted and focus on minimizing their weaknesses. They become expert in those areas where their employees struggle, delicately rename these "skill gaps" or "areas of opportunity," and then pack them off to training classes so that the weaknesses can be fixed. This approach is occasionally necessary: If an employee always alienates those around him, some sensitivity training can help; likewise, a remedial communication class can benefit an employee who happens to be smart but inarticulate. But this isn't development, it is damage control. And by itself damage control is a poor strategy for elevating either the employee or the organization to world-class performance.

As long as an organization operates under these assumptions, it will never capitalize on the strengths of each employee.

To break out of this weakness spiral and to launch the strengths revolution in your own organization, you must change your assumptions about people. Start with the right assumptions, and everything else that follows from them—how you select, measure, train, and develop your people—will be right. These are the two assumptions that guide the world's best managers:

1. Each person's talents are enduring and unique.

2. Each person's greatest room for growth is in the areas of his or her greatest strength.

These two assumptions are the foundation for everything they do with and for their people. These two assumptions explain why great managers are careful to look for talent in every role, why they focus people's performances on outcomes rather than forcing them into a stylistic mold, why they disobey the Golden Rule and treat each employee differently, and why they spend the most time with their best people. In short, these two assumptions explain why the world's best managers break all the rules of conventional management wisdom.

Now, following the great managers' lead, it is time to change the rules. These two revolutionary assumptions must serve as the central tenets for a new way of working. They are the tenets for a new organization, a stronger organization, an organization designed to reveal and stretch the strengths of each employee.

Most organizations have a process for ensuring the efficient use of their practical resources. Six Sigma or ISO 9000 processes are commonplace. Likewise, most organizations have increasingly efficient processes for exploiting their financial resources. The recent fascination with metrics such as economic value added and return on capital bear testament to this. Few organizations, however, have developed a systematic process for the efficient use of their human resources. (They may experiment with individual development plans, 360-degree surveys, and competencies, but these experiments are mostly focused on fixing each employee's weaknesses rather than building his strengths.)

In this book we want to show you how to design a systematic strength-building process. Specifically, Chapter 7, "Building a Strengths-based Organization," can help. Here we describe what the optimum selection system looks like, which three outcomes all employees should have on their scorecard, how to reallocate those misguided training budgets, and, last, how to change the way you channel each employee's career.

If you are a manager and want to know how best to capitalize on the strengths of your individual direct reports, then Chapter 6, "Managing Strengths," will help. Here we identify virtually every ability or style you might find in your people and explain what you can do to maximize the strengths of each employee.

However, we don't start there. We start with you. What are your strengths? How can you capitalize on them? What are your most powerful combinations? Where do they take you? What one, two, or three things can you do better than ten thousand other people? These are the kinds of questions we will deal with in the first five chapters. After all, you can't lead a strengths revolution if you don't know how to find, name, and develop your own.

Two Million Interviews

*"Whom did Gallup interview to learn about
human strengths?"*

Imagine what you might learn if you could interview two million
people about their strengths. Imagine interviewing the world's best
teachers and asking them how they keep children so interested in
what might otherwise be dry subject matter. Imagine asking them
how they build such trusting relationships with so many different
children. Imagine asking them how they balance fun and discipline
in the classroom. Imagine asking them about all the things they do
that make them so very good at what they do.

And then imagine what you could learn if you did the same with
the world's best doctors and salespeople and lawyers (yes, they can
be found) and professional basketball players and stockbrokers and
accountants and hotel housekeepers and leaders and soldiers and
nurses and pastors and systems engineers and chief executives.
Imagine all those questions and, more important, all those vivid
answers.

Over the last thirty years The Gallup Organization has conducted
a systematic study of excellence wherever we could find it. This
wasn't some mammoth poll. Each of those interviews (a little over
two million at the last count, of which the eighty thousand managers
from *First, Break All the Rules* were a small part) consisted of open-
ended questions like the ones mentioned above. We wanted to hear
these excellent performers describe in their own words exactly what
they were doing.

In all these different professions we found a tremendous diversity of knowledge, skill, and talent. But as you might suspect, we
soon began to detect patterns. We kept looking and listening, and
gradually we extracted from this wealth of testimony thirty-four

patterns, or "themes," as we have called them. *These thirty-four are the most prevalent themes of human talent.* Our research tells us that these thirty-four, in their many combinations, can do the best job of explaining the broadest possible range of excellent performance.

These thirty-four do not capture every single human idiosyncrasy—individuals are too infinitely varied for that kind of claim. So think of these thirty-four as akin to the eighty-eight keys on a piano. The eighty-eight keys cannot play every single note that can possibly be played, but in their many combinations they can capture everything from classic Mozart to classic Madonna. The same applies to these thirty-four themes. Used with insight and understanding they can help capture the unique themes playing in each person's life.

To be most helpful we offer you a way to measure yourself on these thirty-four themes. We ask you to pause after reading Chapter 3 and take a profile called StrengthsFinder that is available on the Internet. It will immediately reveal your five dominant themes of talent, your signature themes. These signature themes are your most powerful sources of strength. If you want to learn about the themes of your employees or family or friends, you can read Chapter 4 and learn about each of the thirty-four. But initially our main focus is you. By identifying and refining these signature themes you will be in the best possible position to play out your own strengths to the fullest.

As you study these five themes and consider ways to apply what you have learned, keep this thought in mind: The real tragedy of life is not that each of us doesn't have enough strengths, it's that we fail to use the ones we have. Benjamin Franklin called wasted strengths "sundials in the shade." As you can see, the impetus of this book is that too many organizations, too many teams, and too many individuals unknowingly hide their "sundials in the shade."

We want this book and your experiences while reading it to cast a light and thereby put your strengths to work.

I

The Anatomy of a Strength

CHAPTER 1

Strong Lives

- **THE INVESTOR, THE DIRECTOR, THE SKIN DOCTOR, AND THE EDITOR**

- **TIGER WOODS, BILL GATES, AND COLE PORTER**

- **THREE REVOLUTIONARY TOOLS**

The Investor, the Director, the Skin Doctor, and the Editor

"What does a strong life look like?"

What does a strong life look like? What does it look like when a person succeeds in building his life around his strengths? Let's examine a couple of examples of people who have done so.

* * *

"I am really no different from any of you."

Warren Buffett, with his usual down-home style and slightly disheveled appearance, is talking to a roomful of students at the University of Nebraska. Since he is one of the richest men in the world and since most of the students can barely cover their phone bill, they start to chuckle.

"I may have more money than you do, but money doesn't make the difference. Sure, I can buy the most luxurious handmade suit, but I put it on and it just looks cheap. I would rather have a cheeseburger from Dairy Queen than a hundred-dollar meal." The students seem unconvinced, and so Buffett concedes on one point. "If there is any difference between you and me, it may simply be that I get up every day and have a chance to do what I love to do, every day. If you want to learn anything from me, this is the best advice I can give you."

On the surface this sounds like the kind of glib throwaway line you tell people after you have already banked your first billion. But Buffett is sincere. He loves what he does and genuinely believes that his reputation as the world's greatest investor is due to his ability to carve out a role that plays to his particular strengths.

Surprisingly, his strengths are not those that you might expect to see in a successful investor. Today's global marketplace is fast-paced, extraordinarily complicated, and amoral. Therefore, you would think that the creature best adapted for this world would be blessed with urgency, a conceptual mind to identify patterns in the complex market, and an innate skepticism about everyone else's motives.

Buffett cannot claim any of these strengths. By all accounts he is a patient man. His mind is more practical than conceptual. He is inclined to be trusting of other people's motives, not skeptical. So how did he thrive?

Like many people who are both successful and fulfilled, he found a way to cultivate the strengths he did possess and put them to work. For example, he turned his natural patience into his now-famous "twenty-year perspective" that leads him to invest only in those companies whose trajectory he can forecast with some level of confidence for the next twenty years. His practical mind made him suspicious of investing "theories" and broad market trends. As he said in one Berkshire Hathaway annual report, "The only role of stock forecasters is to make fortune-tellers look good." So he resolved to invest only in those companies whose products and services he could intuitively understand, such as Dairy Queen, The Coca-Cola Company, and The Washington Post Company.

Finally, he put his trusting nature to good use by carefully vetting the senior managers of the companies in which he invested and by stepping back and away, rarely interfering in their day-to-day operations of the business.

Warren Buffett has used this patient, practical, and trusting approach since he formed his first investment partnership with $100 in 1956. He has honed it, perfected it, and stuck to it even when the temptations to adopt a different strategy were tantalizingly sweet. (Remember, he didn't invest in either Microsoft or the Internet because he didn't feel he could paint an accurate picture of where high-tech was going to be in twenty years.) His distinct approach is the cause of his professional success and, to hear him tell it, also the cause of his personal happiness. He is a world-class investor because he deliberately plays to his strengths; he loves what he does because he deliberately plays to his strengths.

In this sense—and perhaps in this sense alone—Warren Buffett is right. He isn't any different from the rest of us. Like the rest of us he responds to the world around him in distinct ways. The way he handles risk, the way he connects with other people, the way he makes his decisions, the way he derives satisfaction—not one of these is random. They all form part of a unique pattern that is so stable his family and closest friends are able to recall its early tracings in the schoolyard in Omaha, Nebraska, half a century ago.

What makes Buffett special is what he did with this pattern. First, he became aware of it. Many of us don't seem able to take even this step. Second, and most significant, he chose not to focus on reinforcing its weaker threads. Instead, he did the exact opposite: He identified its strongest threads, wove in education and experience, and built them into the dominating strengths we see today.

Warren Buffett is relevant here, not because of his personal fortune but because he has figured out something that can serve as a practical guide for all of us. Look inside yourself, try to identify your strongest threads, reinforce them with practice and learning, and then either find or, as he did, carve out a role that draws on these strengths every day. When you do, you will be more productive, more fulfilled, and more successful.

Of course, Buffett isn't the only person to have realized the power of building his life around his strengths. Whenever you interview people who are truly successful at their chosen profession—from teaching to telemarketing, acting to accounting—you discover that the secret to their success lies in their ability to discover their strengths and to organize their life so that these strengths can be applied.

Pam D. is the director of health and human services for an urban county so large that its budget is bigger than twenty American states. Her current challenge is to design and implement an integrated plan for all of the county's programs for seniors. Unfortunately, since neither the county nor the country has ever been faced with the prospect of so many seniors requiring so many services, she has no blueprint to follow. To succeed in this role you might think that Pam would need strengths such as a gift for thinking strategically or, at the very least, for detailed analysis and planning. But although she understands the importance of both, neither comes close to the top of her strengths list.

In fact, two of the strongest threads in her pattern are a need to inject drama and passion into her employees and an impatience for action. Like Buffett she has chosen not to take these threads for granted and work on fixing her weaknesses. Instead, she has carved her role so that she can capitalize on these strong threads most of the time. Her modus operandi is, first, to identify achievable goals where action can be taken today, and act; second, to seek opportunities to paint a picture for her thousands of employees of the overarching purpose of their work; and third, to give the formal strategic planning process to an outside consultant. While she and her team are pushing forward, the consultant can sweep up behind and plug her actions into the "strategic plan."

So far things are working beautifully. She has advanced on all fronts. She has succeeded in winning important service contracts away from the private sector. And she is having a blast.

Sherie S. took a similarly pragmatic approach to building her life around her strengths. Sherie is now a successful doctor, but years ago during medical school she made a rather disturbing discovery: She didn't like being around sick people. Since a doctor who doesn't like sick people seems as incongruous as an investor who doesn't like risk, she began to question her chosen career. Rather than bemoaning her poor choice, however, she took stock of her patterns of thinking and feeling, and gradually came to three realizations: She did indeed enjoy helping people, just not very sick people; she was driven by a constant need for achievement that was best satisfied when she could see tangible and regular proof of progress; these two distinct patterns could prove surprisingly powerful if she made her specialty dermatology.

Now, as a dermatologist, she plays to her strengths every day. Her patients are rarely gravely ill, their illnesses are tangible, and their progress toward recovery is evident on their skin for all to see.

Paula L. didn't have to shift her focus in order to play to her strengths. Instead, like Buffett, she had to remain true to what she already knew about her strengths, despite many alluring temptations to change her tack. Paula is executive editor for one of the most successful women's magazines in the world. As a result of the exposure this position offers her, she has garnered many offers to become editor in chief at other magazines. Naturally, she is flattered by these offers, but she chooses to stay in the executive editor role.

Why? Because she is aware that one of her strongest themes is her conceptual, creative mind. Over the years she has refined this theme into an exceptional strength that enables her to excel as an editor, working with the writers and sub-editors, crafting the actual material that gives the magazine its distinct identity. As the editor in chief of a magazine she would be asked to do less of this. Her time would increasingly be taken up with PR events, and through her choice of clothes, friends, and hobbies, she would be expected to embody the magazine. She knows that she would hate this kind of public scrutiny, so she stays on her strengths' path.

All these people are special in the same sense that Warren Buffett is special. They identified in themselves some recurring patterns of behavior and then figured out a way to develop these patterns into genuine and productive strengths.

Tiger Woods, Bill Gates, and Cole Porter

"What is a strength?"

For the sake of clarity let's be more precise about what we mean by a "strength." The definition of a strength that we will use throughout this book is quite specific: consistent near perfect performance in an activity. By this definition Pam's accurate decision-making and ability to rally people around her organization's common purpose are strengths. Sherie's love of diagnosing and treating skin diseases is a strength. Paula's ability to generate and then refine article ideas that fit her magazine's identity is a strength.

To use more celebrated examples, the golfer Tiger Woods's extraordinary long-game—his length with his woods and his irons—is a strength. As is his putting. His ability to chip out of a bunker—inconsistent when compared to other top professionals (Tiger is 61st on the PGA tour in "sand saves")—is not.

In a business context Bill Gates's genius at taking innovations and transforming them into user-friendly applications is a strength, whereas his ability to maintain and build an enterprise in the face of legal and commercial assault—as compared to his partner's, Steve Ballmer—is not.

In an artistic setting, Cole Porter's ability to carve the perfect lyric was a strength. His attempts at writing believable characters and plots were not.

By defining strength in this way, consistent near perfect performance in an activity, we reveal three of the most important principles of living a strong life.

First, for an activity to be a strength you must be able to do it consistently. And this implies that it is a predictable part of your performance. You may have occasionally hit a shot that would have made Tiger Woods proud, but we are not going to call this activity a strength unless you can demonstrate it time and time again. And you must also derive some intrinsic satisfaction from the activity. Sherie is certainly smart enough to be any kind of doctor, but practicing dermatology constitutes her strength because it is the specialty that energizes her. By contrast, Bill Gates is quite capable of implementing Microsoft's strategy, but because, as he has reported, performing this role drains him of energy, this ability is not a strength. The acid test of a strength? The ability is a strength only if you can fathom yourself doing it repeatedly, happily, and successfully.

Second, you do not have to have strength in every aspect of your role in order to excel. Pam is not the perfect candidate for her role. Neither is Sherie. The people we described above are not exactly suited for their roles. None of them is blessed with the "perfect hand." They are simply doing the best they can with the cards they were dealt. That excellent performers must be well rounded is one of the most pervasive myths we hope to dispel in this book. When we studied them, excellent performers were rarely well rounded. On the contrary, they were sharp.

Third, you will excel only by maximizing your strengths, never by fixing your weaknesses. This is not the same as saying "ignore your weaknesses." The people we described did not ignore their weaknesses. Instead, they did something much more effective. They found ways to manage around their weaknesses, thereby freeing them up to hone their strengths to a sharper point. Each of them did this a little differently. Pam liberated herself by hiring an outside consultant to write the strategic plan. Bill Gates did something similar. He selected a partner, Steve Ballmer, to run the company, allowing him to return to software development and rediscover his strengths' path. Sherie, the dermatologist, simply stopped doing the kind of medicine that drained her. Paula, the magazine editor, turned down job offers.

Tiger Woods was in a slightly tougher spot. He couldn't escape the fact that his bunker play needed to improve, and so, like many of us must, he was forced to do damage control. He worked on his weakness just enough so that it did not undermine his strengths. But once his bunker play reached acceptable levels, he and his coach, Butch Harmon, turned their attention to their most important and creative work: the refining and perfecting of Tiger's most dominant strength, his swing.

Of all of them, Cole Porter pursued the most aggressive and, some might say, riskiest strategy for managing around his weaknesses. He bet that if he kept polishing his strengths as a songwriter, very soon the audience simply wouldn't care that his plots were weak and his characters stereotypical. His strengths would blind people to his weaknesses. Today, many would say that his strategy paid off. When you can write words and melodies as scintillating and sophisticated as his, it is almost irrelevant who is singing them or why.

Each of these people found success and fulfillment in their work in very different fields because they intentionally played to their strengths. We want to help you do the same—*to capitalize on your strengths,* whatever they may be, *and manage around your weaknesses,* whatever they may be.

Three Revolutionary Tools

*"What do you need to build your life around
your strengths?"*

This advice, "capitalize on your strengths and manage around your weaknesses," is easy to grasp. But as you probably know from experience, it is hard to apply. After all, building a strong life will always be a challenging assignment involving a myriad of different variables: your self-awareness, your maturity, your opportunities, the people with whom you surround yourself, the people from whom you can't seem to escape. To be clear at the outset, we need to tell you what this book can and cannot provide as you build a new, strengths-based image of yourself.

We cannot show you the completed image; even if we did, the picture would be instantly inaccurate since each of us is never completed. Nor can we tell you how to learn. As you are doubtless aware, it will always be your responsibility to take the action, ponder the repercussion, and slide the learning into place. No one else can do that for you.

However, what we can offer you are the three revolutionary tools you will need to build a strong life:

1. **The first revolutionary tool is understanding how to distinguish your natural talents from things you can learn.** We have defined a strength as consistent near perfect performance in an activity. All right, but how do you get there? Can you reach near perfect performance in any activity you choose just as long as you practice and practice, or does near perfect performance require certain natural talents?

If you struggle to build a network of people who are prepared to go out of their way to help you, can you become an excellent net-worker with practice? If you find it difficult to anticipate, can you learn to devise perfectly crafted strategies? If you often find your-self unable to confront people directly, can you with discipline and practice become extraordinarily persuasive?

The question isn't whether or not you can improve at these activities. Of course you can. Human beings are adaptable creatures, and if it is important enough for us, we can get a little better at virtually anything. The question is whether you can reach consistent near perfect performance in these activities through practice alone. The answer to this question is "No, practice doesn't necessarily make perfect." To develop a strength in any activity requires certain natural talents.

This raises some slippery questions. What is the difference between a talent and a strength? Which aspects of a strength in net-working or strategizing or persuading can be learned, and which aspects are innate? What role do skills, knowledge, experience, and self-awareness play in building a strength? If you don't know how to come to grips with these questions, you may waste a great deal of time trying to learn strengths that aren't learnable, or, conversely, you may give up too early on strengths that are.

To answer these questions you need a simple way to differenti-ate between what is innate and what you can acquire with practice. In the next chapter we present a practical way to do this. Specifically, we introduce you to three carefully defined terms:

- *Talents* are your naturally recurring patterns of thought, feeling, or behavior. Your various themes of talent are what the StrengthsFinder Profile actually measures.

- *Knowledge* consists of the facts and lessons learned.

- *Skills* are the steps of an activity.

These three—talents, knowledge, and skills—combine to create your strengths.

For example, to be drawn toward strangers and to enjoy the challenge of making a connection with them is a talent (defined later in the book as the theme "Woo"), whereas the ability to build a network of supporters who know you and are prepared to help you is a strength. To build this strength you have perfected your innate talent with skills and knowledge. Likewise, to be able to confront others is a talent (defined later as the theme "Command"), whereas the ability to sell successfully is a strength. To persuade others to buy your product you must have combined your talent with product knowledge and certain selling skills.

Although all are important to strength building, of these three raw materials the most important are talents. Your talents are innate (we'll explain why in the next chapter), whereas skills and knowledge can be acquired through learning and practice; for example, as a salesperson you can learn how to describe your products' features (knowledge), you can even learn how to ask the right open-ended questions to elicit each prospect's needs (a skill), but you'll never learn how to push that prospect to commit at exactly the right moment and in exactly the right way. These are talents (defined later as the themes "Command" and "Individualization").

Although it is occasionally possible to build a strength without acquiring the relevant knowledge and skills—there are "natural" salespeople who have so much innate talent for persuasion that they can sell even though their knowledge of the product is rather limited—it is never possible to possess a strength without the requisite talent. In many roles you can acquire the relevant knowledge and skills to the point where you are able to get by, but no matter what the role, if you lack the necessary talents, you will never be able to have consistent near perfect performance.

Thus, the key to building a bona fide strength is to identify your dominant talents and then refine them with knowledge and skills.

Remember that many people don't appreciate what talents are, let alone what *their* talents are. They think that with enough practice almost everything is learnable. They don't actively seek knowledge and skills to enhance their talents. Rather, they fall into the trap of trying to acquire as much knowledge and as many skills as they are able in the hope of bettering themselves in some general way, smoothing out their rough edges, and emerging suitably well rounded.

To build your strengths you must avoid this trap. Don't sign up blindly for leadership skills training or listening skills or empathy skills or public speaking skills or assertiveness skills or any of those well-meaning classes and expect dramatic improvement. Unless you have the necessary talent, your improvements will be modest. You will be diverting most of your energy toward damage control and very little toward real development. And since you have only a finite amount of time to invest in yourself, you have to decide whether a fixation on damage control will net you the best return.

We suggest you take a close look at knowledge, skills, and talents. Learn to distinguish each one from the others. Identify your dominant talents and then in a focused way acquire the knowledge and skills to turn them into real strengths.

2. **The second revolutionary tool is a system to identify your dominant talents.** There is one sure way to identify your greatest potential for strength: Step back and watch yourself for a while. Try an activity and see how quickly you pick it up, how quickly you skip steps in the learning and add twists and kinks you haven't been taught yet. See whether you become absorbed in the activity to such an extent that you lose track of time. If none of these has happened after a couple of months, try another activity and watch—and another. Over time your dominant talents will reveal themselves, and you can start to refine them into a powerful strength.

This is probably what school should be like: a focused hunt for a child's areas of greatest potential. This is probably what work should be like: an intentional effort to find out how each employee might approach world-class performance levels. Unfortunately, neither school nor work seems up to the task. Both are so preoccupied with transferring knowledge and plugging skill gaps that developing awareness of natural talents is disregarded. And so the burden falls on you, the individual. You must lead the search for your own talents.

The StrengthsFinder Profile discussed in Chapter 4 is designed to help you identify your dominant talents. It will not attempt to define you completely or label you as this type or that, strong here and weak there. Each of us is too nuanced for that kind of simplification. StrengthsFinder's purpose is more focused. It is designed to reveal your five strongest themes of talent. These themes may not be strengths yet. They are areas of greatest potential, areas in which you have the best possible chance to cultivate a world-class strength. StrengthsFinder will shine a spotlight on them. It will be up to you to perform.

3. **The third revolutionary tool is a common language to describe your talents.** We need a new language to help explain the strengths we see in ourselves and others. This language must be precise; it must be able to describe the subtle ways in which one person differs from another. It must be positive; it must help us explain *strength,* not frailty. And it must be common; it must be a language in which we are all fluent so that no matter who we are or where we are from, we all know exactly what is meant when someone says, "Marcus embodies Command" or "Don exhibits Achiever."

Why do we need this new language? Quite simply because the language we currently use isn't up to the challenge.

The language of human weakness is rich and varied. There are meaningful differences in the terms neurosis, psychosis, depression, mania, hysteria, panic attacks, and schizophrenia. An expert in mental illness is acutely aware of these differences and takes them into consideration in making a diagnosis and determining treatment. In fact, this language of frailty is so widespread that most of us non-experts probably use it pretty accurately.

By contrast, the language of human strength is sparse. If you want to know just how sparse, listen to a couple of human resources professionals describing the merits of three candidates for a position. You might hear a couple of broad generalizations such as "I liked her people skills" or "He seemed self-motivated," but then the conversation will revert to comparisons of facts such as each candidate's education and work experience. We don't mean to single out human resources professionals. If you listen to senior managers discussing the same three people, you will probably hear a similar conversation. More than likely the candidates, when trying to describe their own strengths, will roll out the same generalizations and then dive into the comfortable certainty of their education and work experience.

The sorry truth is that the language available, the language of human strength, is still rudimentary at best. Take the term "people skills" as an example. If you say that two people have "people skills," what does that tell you about them? It tells you they both seem to relate well with people, but probably not much else. It doesn't tell you, for example, that one excels at building trust with people once the initial contact has been made, while the other is brilliant at initiating the contact. Both of these abilities have to do with people, but they are obviously not the same. Yet this difference has practical implications. Regardless of experience or education, you wouldn't necessarily put the great trust builder in the same role as the great networker. Nor would you expect them to connect with customers and associates in the same way. Nor would you expect them to derive the same kind of satisfaction from their work. Nor would you necessarily manage them in the same way. Since these variables combine to create each one's performance, knowing who is the instinctive trust builder and who is the networker might make the difference between success and failure. In this situation the term "people skills" simply doesn't help you very much.

Unfortunately, this applies to most of the language of human strengths. What does "self-motivated" mean exactly? Does it mean that the person is driven by an internal need for achievement that will keep firing away no matter how you manage her? Or does it mean that she needs you to set challenging goals, which she then motivates herself to surpass? What does a "strategic thinker" mean? Does it mean he is conceptual and loves theories? Or does it imply that he is analytical and loves proof? What about "selling skills"? If someone has them, does this mean that she closes by going for the jugular, by wooing, by logical persuasion, or by expressing fervent belief in the product? These are important distinctions if you want to match the right salesperson with the right prospects.

It is possible that you know exactly what you mean by "selling skills," "strategic thinking," "people skills," and "self-motivated." But what about the people around you? They may use the same words but give them very different meanings. This is the worst kind of miscommunication. You finish the conversation and think you are both on the same page when in fact you aren't even speaking the same language.

And for some strange reason when we do have a precise, commonly agreed upon word for a strong pattern of behavior, the word we use often has a negative connotation. Remember Pam D., the health and human services director who can't wait to act? She is impatient or impulsive.

People who are brilliant at imposing order and structure on the world? Anal.

People who claim excellence? Egotists.

People who anticipate and are always asking "What if?" Worriers.

Whichever way you look at it, we don't have a rich enough language to describe the wealth of human talent we see around us.

In Chapter 4 we will introduce the thirty-four themes of talent. Obviously, these are not the only words that describe patterns of behavior, but they are the words that captured the most prevalent patterns in our study of excellence. These thirty-four themes have become our language for describing human talents and, thereby, for explaining human strengths. We offer them to you as a way of revealing the best in you and the best in those around you.

CHAPTER **2**

Strength Building

- **IS HE ALWAYS THIS GOOD?**

- **KNOWLEDGE AND SKILLS**

- **TALENT**

Is He Always This Good?

"What can we learn about strengths from Colin Powell?"

Recently, General Colin Powell came to speak to one thousand of The Gallup Organization's leaders. His reputation was almost ridiculously impressive. We knew him to be the former national security advisor, chairman of the Joint Chiefs of Staff, commander-in-chief of NATO's forces during Desert Shield and Desert Storm, and, according to the last decade of global polls, one of the ten most respected leaders in the world. Needless to say, our expectations were high. As he walked onstage after a suitably glowing introduction, more than a few of us wondered whether the performance would live up to the resume.

By the end of the speech we had a different question: "Is he always this good?" In the course of one short hour General Powell had revealed himself to be an especially gifted public speaker. He drew us into the intimate politics of President Ronald Reagan's Oval Office. He placed us across a table in the Kremlin as Mikhail Gorbachev announced perestroika with: "General, you are going to have to find yourself another enemy." He had us waiting by the phone for General H. Norman Schwarzkopf's call to report on the first air strikes of Desert Storm. He spoke casually, without the formulaic patter of the politician, without the bombast of the preacher, without structure, and without notes. He just had a few stories to tell, and as he talked, almost accidentally these stories laced themselves together into a narrative about leadership and character. It was a simple message, perfectly delivered.

A strength such as this is intimidating. For the audience, the General's performance stood far above basic analysis. We didn't want to ask, "Where did he learn this?" because it was quite obvious that neither Toast Masters nor Dale Carnegie had anything to do with his performance. Instead, we wanted to know "Where did this come from?" as though the performance was not being created by General Powell but was being channeled through him, flawless and sublime.

All strengths have this quality. Stand in front of a Monet for a few moments, and it appears complete, like a circle. You don't imagine a tentative beginning, a slew of clumsy crossings-out in the middle, and a last brush stroke to finish the painting. You experience it as a whole, all-at-once perfection.

The strength doesn't have to be artistic to be intimidating. Any near perfect performance stimulates this same feeling of awe. A friend tells a joke with timing and flare, and you wonder "How did he do that?". A colleague writes a client letter that is both focused and intriguing, and you ask yourself the same thing.

And it is not just the "near perfect" aspect of a strength that so impresses us; the "consistent" part is equally amazing. Cal Ripken played in 2,216 consecutive baseball games. How did he manage that? Bettina K., one of Disney World's best housekeepers, has cleaned the same section of rooms in the same hotel for more than twenty-one years. How does she stick with it? Before his death in February 2000, Charles Schulz had drawn the same cartoon strip, Peanuts, for over forty-one years. How did he do that?

Whether the question is "How does he do it so well?" or "How does he do it for so long?" any consistently near perfect performance seems almost too amazing to analyze. But, of course, strengths do not emerge perfect and whole. Each person's strengths are *created*—developed from some very specific raw materials. You can acquire some materials, your knowledge and skills, with practice and learning; others, your talents, you simply have to hone.

Knowledge and Skills

"Which aspects of you can you change?"

KNOWLEDGE

The exact definition of "knowledge" has withstood centuries of philosophical assault, and we don't want to join in the fray. So let's step around it. Let's just say that, *for the purposes of building your strengths,* there are two distinct kinds of knowledge. You need both, and, fortunately, both can be acquired.

First, you need factual knowledge, which is content. For example, when you start to learn a language, factual knowledge is the vocabulary. You must learn what each word means, or you will never be able to speak the language. In the same vein, salespeople must spend time learning their products' features. Mobile telephone customer service representatives must know the benefits that each calling plan confers. Pilots must learn the call sign protocols. Nurses must know exactly how much Novocain is appropriate for each procedure.

Factual knowledge such as this won't guarantee excellence, but excellence is impossible without it. Thus, no matter what your skills or talents, you will never excel at painting if you don't know that red and green paint, when combined, create the color brown. Likewise, all the creativity in the world is not going to help you excel at lighting design if you don't know that red and green light, when combined, don't create the color brown. Red light and green light make yellow light.

Factual knowledge such as this gets you into the game.

The second kind of knowledge you need is experiential, which isn't taught in classrooms or found in manuals. Rather, it is something that you must discipline yourself to pick up along the way and retain.

Some of it is practical. For example, Katie M., a producer of segments for a morning television show, initially struggled to produce clear and compelling two-minute pieces. She gradually realized that she was ignoring the most important rule of journalism: Always set the stage. Regardless of how creative the rest of the piece was, if the audience wasn't told immediately whom they were watching and why, they would quickly tune out.

Andy Kaufman, the comic captured by Jim Carrey in the film *Man on the Moon,* picked up something similar about the importance of stage setting. At the beginning of his career he was experimenting with two characters: Foreign Man, a sweet, naive straight man, and an Elvis Presley impression. Both characters got a few laughs but nothing spectacular until, as Andy said, "In college I saw that the audience wouldn't accept it if I started out with Elvis Presley. They were offended. They'd go, 'What, he thinks he's handsome or something?' I decided that my natural innocence had been lost after the first few times I did my act. I thought I could be more innocent as the Foreign Man. . . . So the first time I tried it, the whole act was Foreign Man, and when I got to the Elvis part, I said, 'So now I vould like to do de Elvis Presley.' " From the uproar in the audience he could see immediately that he was on the right track.

Both of these examples concern the way a performance is staged, but as you can imagine, experiential knowledge takes a multitude of forms. The salesperson discovers that the first and most important sale she makes is the prospect's assistant. The marketing executive notices that if you want to sell to mothers, radio ads work a lot better than television ads (for busy mothers the radio is a more constant companion than the television). Both of these people have picked up an important tidbit of knowledge, and each now performs better as a result.

Every environment offers chances to learn. Clearly, to develop your strengths it is your responsibility to keep alert for these opportunities and then to incorporate them into your performance.

Some experiential knowledge is more conceptual. Take the most obvious examples: your values and your self-awareness. Both of these need to be refined if you are to build your strengths, and, again, both of them can be developed over time. In fact, often when we say, "So-and-so has changed," we don't really mean that his underlying personality has changed but that his value system has changed or that his comfort with who he is has changed.

Charles Colson, special counsel to President Richard Nixon, was jailed because his excessive loyalty led him to commit crimes to protect his president. Today he is a born-again Christian. Has he changed? Here is Winifred Gallagher's answer in her book *Just the Way You Are*: "Charles Colson would have beat his grandmother to death when he was with Nixon, but then he was born again. He probably always had a very emotional, intense temperament, but now he has different enemies and friends. His nature didn't change—he just does something else with all that zeal. One's mode of engagement with life may not alter much. But one's focus can . . ."

Wherever we look, we can see examples of people who changed their focus by changing their values: Saul's religious conversion on the road to Damascus; the charity work of the disgraced British cabinet minister John Profumo and the American junk-bond king Michael Milken; the animal-rights activism of the notorious rocker Ozzy Osbourne; the remorse of Hitler's architect Albert Speer; and perhaps the most impressive example, the courageous transformations achieved by millions of members of Alcoholics Anonymous.

These examples are uplifting in the sense that they offer each of us the hope of redemption. But uplifting though they may be, we should bear in mind that these people did not change their basic nature or, as we will define later, their talents. They simply redirected their talents toward very different and more positive ends. Thus, the lesson we should draw from these people is not that each person's talents are infinitely malleable or that they can be anything they want to be if they just apply themselves. Rather, the lesson is that talents, like intelligence, are value neutral. If you want to change your life so that others may benefit from your strengths, then change your values. Don't waste time trying to change your talents.

The same applies to self-awareness. Over time each of us becomes more and more aware of who we really are. This growing awareness of self is vital to strength building because it allows each of us to identify more clearly our natural talents and to cultivate these talents into strengths. Unfortunately, this process is not always smooth. Some of us identify our talents accurately enough but then wish we were blessed with different ones. Like Mozart's rival, Salieri, in the film *Amadeus,* we become increasingly bitter as we try and fail to conjure new talents from within. When we are in this mode, we aren't much fun to be around. No matter how many classes we take, no matter how many books we read, it still grates, it is still hard, and it still doesn't seem to get any easier. If you have ever found yourself in a role that asked you to be something you are not, you know how this feels.

And then suddenly we have a revelation. "I should never have taken this sales job. I hate bothering people." Or maybe "I'm not a manager! I much prefer doing my own work than being responsible for other people's." We return to our strengths path, and our friends, impressed by all the good things that happen as a result—our productivity increase, our attitude improvement—look at us and say, "Wow, look at him. He changed."

Well, no, the exact opposite has happened. What looks on the surface like transformation is actually acceptance of some things that can never be transformed—talents. We don't change. We simply accept our talents and refocus our lives around them. We become more self-aware.

In order to build your strengths, you will need to do the same.

SKILLS

Skills bring structure to experiential knowledge. What does this mean? It means that, whatever the activity, at some point a smart person will sit back and formalize all the accumulated knowledge into a sequence of steps that, if followed, will lead to performance—not necessarily great performance but acceptable performance nonetheless.

To illustrate, let's return to General Powell for a moment. After studying General Powell and other public speakers, this smart person will realize that great speakers always seem to start by telling the audience what they are going to say. Then they proceed to do exactly that. Then they close by reminding the audience about what they have heard. This sequence becomes the most basic skill of public speaking:

1. Always start by telling people what you are going to tell them.

2. Tell them.

3. Tell them what you have told them.

Follow this sequence of steps, and you will be a better public speaker.

If our smart person studies a little more, he will soon realize that General Powell, as with other great speakers, was not speaking extemporaneously. On the contrary, he knew exactly what stories he was going to tell, and more than likely he had practiced those stories out loud by himself, playing with the words, the emphasis, the timing. Our smart person might then take this insight and formalize it into the second skill of public speaking.

1. Write down any story or fact or example that resonates with you.

2. Practice telling it out loud. Listen to yourself actually saying the words.

3. These stories will become your "beads," as in the beads of a necklace.

4. All you have to do when giving a speech is string your beads in the appropriate order, and you will give a speech that seems as natural as conversation.

5. Use 3-by-5 cards or a clipping file to keep adding new beads to your string.

Skills enable you to avoid trial and error and to incorporate directly into your performance the best discoveries from the best performers. If you want to build your strengths, whether in selling, marketing, financial analysis, flying, or healing, you will need to learn and practice all the relevant skills available.

But be careful. Skills are so enticingly helpful that they obscure their two flaws. The first flaw is that while skills will help you perform, they will not help you excel. If you learn the skills of public speaking, you may wind up being a better public speaker than you were before, but lacking the necessary talents, you will never be as good as General Powell. The General is blessed with a talent that enables him to become *more* articulate when he is onstage. Somehow his brain filters the faces of the people in front of him and brings him more words, better words, fast. Without this talent you might follow the step-by-step sequence of the skill but still struggle to deliver a sublime performance. Thus, in the same way that learning the grammar of language will not help you write beautiful prose, learning a skill will not necessarily lead to near perfect performance in any activity. Without underlying talent, learning a skill is a survival technique, not a path to glory.

The second flaw is that some activities, almost by definition, defy being broken down into steps. Take empathy, for example. Empathy is the talent to pick up on the feelings of other people. No matter how smart you are, can you really break empathy down into a series of measured steps? Surely empathy happens in the moment. As you talk to someone, you notice a minuscule pause before he mentions someone's name. You instinctively realize that he has paused every time he was about to mention this person's name. You ask about this person, and when responding, he is a little too effusive. It's something in his voice. He is one decibel too loud, one tone too positive. And just then your brain hands the explanation to you: He is deeply upset with this person.

This is what real empathy is like—immediate, instantaneous, instinctive. When you think about it, this is what real assertiveness is like. This is what real strategic thinking is like. This is what real creativity is like. No matter how smart the observer, no matter how well intentioned, he is not going to be able to break these activities down into preplanned steps. In fact, as you may have experienced, his efforts to do so may actually end up confusing you.

The bottom line on skills is this: A skill is designed to make the secrets of the best easily transferable. If you learn a skill, it will help you get a little better, but it will not cover for a lack of talent. Instead, as you build your strengths, skills will actually prove most valuable when they are combined with genuine talent.

Talent

"Which aspects of you are enduring?"

We have been invoking the word "talent" for the last few pages. Now it's time to investigate it more fully. What is talent? Why are your talents enduring and unique? And why are your talents so important to strength building? Let's take these questions one by one.

What is talent?
Talent is often described as "a special natural ability or aptitude," but for the purposes of strength building we suggest a more precise and comprehensive definition, which is derived from our studies of great managers. Talent is any recurring pattern of thought, feeling, or behavior that can be productively applied. Thus, if you are instinctively inquisitive, this is a talent. If you are competitive, this is a talent. If you are charming, this is a talent. If you are persistent, this is a talent. If you are responsible, this is a talent. *Any* recurring pattern of thought, feeling, or behavior is a talent if this pattern can be productively applied.

By this definition even seemingly negative traits can be called talents if they can be productively applied. Obstinacy? Being obstinate is a talent if you find yourself in a role where sticking to your guns in the face of overwhelming resistance is a prerequisite for success—a sales role, for example, or a lawyer in a courtroom. Nervousness? Being nervous is a talent if it causes you to ask yourself "What if?" and to anticipate potential pitfalls and design contingency plans. This kind of scenario planning can prove very productive in a variety of roles.

Even a "frailty" such as dyslexia is a talent if you can figure out a way to apply it productively. David Boies is dyslexic. Boies was the United States government's lawyer in its antitrust suit against the software giant Microsoft. He was the one who wore down Bill Gates with his persistently polite questioning during the pretrial deposition and who won over the judge with his clear exposition of the government's case. His dyslexia causes him to shy away from long, complicated words. He knows what these words mean but doesn't use them in his arguments because, as he described in a recent interview, "I am afraid that I will mispronounce them." Happily, this need to rely on simple words makes his arguments very easy to follow. Furthermore, without his necessarily intending it, he comes across as a commonsensical man of the people. His straightforward language sends the message "I don't know any more than you. I am simply trying to get my head around a difficult subject, just as you are."

For David Boies dyslexia is a talent because he has figured out a way to apply this recurring pattern productively and, by combining it with knowledge and skills, to turn it into a strength.

This is obviously an extreme and rare example, but it serves to make the point: Your talents are those recurring patterns of thought, feeling, or behavior that you can productively apply.

Why are your talents enduring and unique?

What creates in you these recurring patterns? If you don't much care for your patterns, can you stitch a new design? The answers to these questions are (a) your recurring patterns are created by the connections in your brain; and (b) no, beyond a certain age you are not going to be able to stitch a completely new design—your talents are enduring.

Given the large sums of money that companies spend on remediation programs, in effect trying to reconfigure people's brains for empathy or competitiveness or strategic thinking, we had better explain (b). Fortunately, (a) explains (b). If you know how your brain's threads are woven, you know why they are so hard to reweave. So let's look more closely at (a).

The brain is an odd organ in that it seems to grow backward.

Your liver, your kidneys, and, thankfully, your skin all start small and become gradually larger until they reach the appropriate adult size. With your brain, the opposite happens. Your brain gets very big very quickly and then shrinks and shrinks into adulthood. Most bizarre of all, as your brain becomes smaller and smaller, you become smarter and smarter.

The secret to making sense of this topsy-turvy organ can be found in what is called a "synapse." A synapse is a connection between two brain cells that enables the cells (also called neurons) to communicate with one another. These synapses are your threads, and you need to know about them because, as it says in one neurology textbook, "Behavior depends on the formation of appropriate interconnections among neurons in the brain."

Put more plainly, your synapses create your talents.

So how are your synaptic connections made? Forty-two days after you are conceived, your brain experiences a four-month growth spurt. Actually, the word "spurt" doesn't do justice to the sheer scale of what happens. On your forty-second day you create your first neuron, and 120 days later you have a hundred billion of them. That's a staggering 9,500 new neurons every second. But once this explosion dies down, much of the neuron drama is over. You have a hundred billion when you are born, and you have about that many up until late middle age.

Elsewhere in your brain, however, the real drama, the synapse drama, is just beginning. Sixty days before your birth your neurons start trying to communicate with one another. Each neuron reaches out—literally "reaches out" a strand called an axon—and attempts to make a connection. Whenever a successful connection is made, a synapse is formed, and during the first three years of your life, your neurons prove phenomenally successful at making these connections. In fact, by the age of three each of your hundred billion neurons has formed fifteen thousand synaptic connections with other neurons. Just to be clear, that's fifteen thousand connections for *each* of your hundred billion neurons. Your pattern of threads, extensive, intricate, and unique, is woven.

But then something strange happens. For some reason nature now prompts you to ignore a lot of your carefully woven threads. As with most things, threads that are neglected fall into disrepair, and so across your network connections start to break. You become so inattentive to parts of your mental network that between the ages of three and fifteen you lose billions and billions of these carefully forged synaptic connections. By the time you wake up on your sixteenth birthday, half your network is gone.

And the bad news is that you can't rebuild it. Yes, over the course of your life your brain does retain some of its early plasticity. For example, it now appears that learning and memory require the formation of new synaptic connections, as does figuring out how to cope with the loss of a limb or your eyesight. However, for most practical purposes, the configuration of your mental network, with its range of stronger to weaker connections, doesn't change much after your mid-teens.

This all sounds very odd. Why would nature do this? Why would it expend so much energy creating this network only to let large chunks of it wither and die? The answer to this question, as educator John Bruer describes in his book *The Myth of the First Three Years,* is that when it comes to the brain, "less is more." Parents hang black-and-white mobiles and play Mozart CDs in the crib in order to stimulate synapse creation in their child, but they are missing the point. It is not true that the more synaptic connections you have, the smarter you are or the more effective. Rather, your smartness and your effectiveness depend on how well you capitalize on your strongest connections. Nature forces you to shut down billions of connections precisely so that you can be freed up to exploit the ones remaining. Losing connections isn't something to be concerned about. Losing connections is the point.

Initially, nature gives you more connections than you will ever need because during those first few years, you have a great deal to soak up. But soaking up is all you are doing. You are not yet making sense of your world. You can't because with this abundance of connections you are overwhelmed by so many signals from so many different directions. To make sense of your world you will have to shut out some of this noise in your head. Nature helps you do just that over the next decade. Your genetic inheritance and early childhood experiences assist you in finding some connections smoother and easier to use than others—the competitive connection, perhaps, or the inquisitiveness connection or the strategic thinking connection. You are drawn to these connections time and time again until they become tighter and tauter. To use an Internet analogy, these are your superfast T1 lines. Here the signals are loud and strong.

Meanwhile, ignored and unused, other connections in other parts of your network wither away. No signal at all can be heard. For example, if you end up with a T1 line for competitiveness, when you see numbers, you cannot help using them to compare your performance with other people's. Or if you wind up with a T1 line for inquisitiveness, you are the kind of person who can't help asking why. At the other extreme, you may lose your center-of-attention connection. Unlike General Powell, your brain freezes when you feel the eyes of the audience on you. Or perhaps you have no connection for empathy. Rationally, you understand that empathy is important, but moment by moment you just can't seem to pick up the signals that other people are sending.

On a microscopic level your mental network, ranging from smooth T1 lines all the way to broken connections, explains why certain behaviors and reactions "just feel right" to you, while others, no matter how hard you practice, always seem stilted and forced. This is as it should be. If nature didn't whittle down your network to a smaller number of strongly forged connections, you would never become an adult. You would remain a permanent child, frozen in sensory overload.

Author Jorge Borges imagined what such a character might be like. He told of a boy "possessed of an infinite memory. Nothing escapes him; all of his sensory experience, past and present, persists in his mind; drowned in particulars, unable to forget the changing formations of all the clouds he has seen, he cannot form general ideas, and therefore . . . cannot think." A boy like this wouldn't be able to feel, either, or build relationships or make decisions of any kind. He would lack personality, preference, judgment, and passion. He would be talentless.

To save you from this fate, nature and nurture reinforce some connections and allow billions of others to fade away. And so you emerge—a distinctly talented individual blessed and/or cursed to react to the world in your own enduringly unique way.

Many of us may find it hard to convince ourselves of this enduring uniqueness. Our talents come so easily to us that we acquire a false sense of security: Doesn't everyone see the world as I do? Doesn't everyone feel a sense of impatience to get this project started? Doesn't everyone want to avoid conflict and find the common ground? Can't everyone see the obstacles lying in wait if we proceed down this path? Our talents feel so natural to us that they seem to be common sense. On some level it is quite comforting to believe that the "sense" we make of the world is "common" to everyone.

But in truth our sense isn't common at all. The sense we make of the world is individual. Our "sense," our recurring pattern of thought, feeling, or behavior, is caused by our unique mental network. This network serves as a filter, sorting and sifting the world we encounter, causing us to zero in on some stimuli and miss others entirely.

To illustrate this, imagine that you are sitting down for dinner with five acquaintances in a favorite restaurant. Let's say that you are blessed with the talent of empathy, so in situations such as this your mental filter causes you to wonder how everyone is feeling tonight. You smile at each person, ask a few questions, and instinctively start tuning your frequency to pick up the emotional signals emanating from each one. And as you look around the table, it is tempting—and, to be frank, easier—to assume that roughly the same thoughts are running through everyone's mind.

But of course they aren't. One of your companions has apologized for showing up late and is wondering whether he should offer to pay for dinner by way of restitution. As we shall describe later, this is the talent of Responsibility. Another is trying to guess what each person will be ordering tonight—the talent of Individualization. Another is hoping that she will manage to squeeze into the seat next to her closest friend so that she will have a chance to "really catch up"—the talent of Relator, of building in-depth relationships. Still another is worried that two of the party will start arguing "like the last time we all went out" and so is figuring out ways to steer the conversation away from volatile subjects—the talent of Harmony, of building consensus. Your last dinner companion is oblivious to all this and is mentally rehearsing a funny story that he hopes to tell later—the talent of Communication, of finding drama in words.

Five friends in the same situation, each filtering it in ways radically different from your own. In a social context these unique filters can help explain why the six of you have such lively conversations and why each person seems just a little mysterious to the others. In a work context the fact that each person's filter is unique provides rather more practical explanations. For example, have you ever tried and failed to persuade someone, using simple and easy-to-understand language, to see things your way? It can be very frustrating. You told him how it is, you laid things out clearly and convincingly, and yet he still wandered off and did something completely different. Wasn't he listening? If he didn't agree, why didn't he just say so? Why must you keep having the same conversation with him over and over?

It is obvious now that the answer to all these questions is not that he wasn't listening or that he was being deliberately contrary. The answer is that he couldn't look through your eyes. His filter didn't allow him to. He understood your words, but he couldn't see your world. Imagine trying to explain the color purple to someone who is color-blind, and you will get an idea of what is happening with that person. No matter how eloquent your description of purple, he will never see it.

Perhaps this overstates our inherent separation from one another. Obviously, we are not totally isolated by our uniqueness. Each of us shares many of the same thoughts and feelings as our fellow man. Regardless of the culture in which we were raised, each of us is familiar with emotions such as fear, pain, shame, and pride. In his recent book *How the Mind Works,* Steven Pinker, the Massachusetts Institute of Technology professor, describes a famous experiment, which debunks the notion that individuals from different cultures have radically different personalities. A couple of sociologists showed New Guinean highlanders a series of photographs of Stanford University students. Each photograph depicted an American student's face in the throes of an extreme emotion: happiness, love, disgust, or pain. The sociologists then asked the highlanders to name the emotion behind each face. Despite their lack of familiarity with photographs in general and with Anglo-American features in particular, they recognized every single emotion.

On some level this is a pleasing discovery. It reinforces the notion that no matter what our cultural heritage, we can indeed relate to one another. However, discoveries such as these do not refute what we have been saying about the uniqueness of each individual's filter. The boundaries of human experience are finite (if you haven't experienced emotions such as pain or fear or shame, you are either a sociopath or an alien), but within these boundaries there is significant range and diversity. Regardless of race, sex, or age, some people love pressure and some people hate it, some strive for significance and some live comfortably in the crowd, some revel in confrontation and some yearn for harmony.

The most interesting differences between people are rarely a function of race or sex or age; they are a function of each person's network of mental connections. As an individual employee responsible both for your performance and for directing your own career, it is vital that you gain an accurate understanding of how your mental connections are grooved. As a manager you must take the time to identify the distinct talents of your staff. In the next chapter, with the help of some clues to talent and the StrengthsFinder Profile itself, we will help you do this. But before we do, one last question begs an answer.

Why are your talents so important to strength building?

The acid test of a strength is that you can do it consistently and nearly perfectly. By defining your talents as your strongest synaptic connections, we can now see why it is impossible to build a strength without underlying talent.

Every day at work you have decisions to make. Your talents, your mental T1 lines, dominate the decision-making. Our concern here is not with the major decisions such as whether to relocate a factory from the United States to Europe or whether to move someone from sales into marketing. Our concern is with the thousands of small decisions that confront you throughout the day. While sitting at your desk, you look at the files spread out in front of you. Which one should you open? The one that requires very little work or the tough one that might take the whole morning to complete? You open the latter. You are like that. You prefer to tackle the difficult work first. Then the phone rings. Do you ignore it, preferring to stay focused on the task at hand, or do you pick it up? If you pick it up, do you recognize the person's voice? Do you remember his name? What tone of voice do you use? If he confronts you with a challenge, do you immediately defend yourself, or do you allow him to get everything off his chest? One after another, in an endless procession, these small choices present themselves.

Unable to intellectualize every minute decision, you are compelled to react instinctively. Your brain does what nature always does in situations such as this: It finds and follows the path of least resistance, your talents. A choice appears, you are immediately whisked away down one of your T1 lines, and—bam—the decision is made. Another choice. Another trip down a T1 line. Another decision.

The sum of these tiny decisions—let's say a thousand a day—is your performance for the day. Multiply this number by five, and you get your performance for the week. Multiply by, let's say, 240 working days, and you have your performance for the year. Roughly 240,000 decisions, and your talents, your strongest synaptic connections, made almost every one of them.

That explains why it is virtually impossible to create near perfect performance by simply teaching someone a new skill. As we described earlier, when you learn a skill, what you learn are the steps of an activity. With the learning you may weave a few new connections, but you do *not* learn how to reweave your entire network. The new skill you just acquired may be able to intervene in a few decisions and redirect you down one of your weaker connections, but only a few. The decisions are too numerous and too immediate for the skill to block off your T1 lines completely and create a consistent and significant change in your behavior. Skills determine if you *can* do something, whereas talents reveal something more important: *how well and how often you do it.*

For example, if you lack the talent of empathy but have attended an empathy skills class, you may now know that you are supposed to be on the lookout for emotional cues or that you should repeat back to the person your understanding of what has been said so he can feel "heard." During the heat of the conversation, however, your brain may keep channeling you down your T1 lines, which unfortunately are not those dealing with empathy. So you interrupt when you should be "reflecting back." You look away when you should be "maintaining eye contact." You find yourself shuffling in your seat even though your body language is supposed to be "open and accepting." Occasionally your rational mind may remind you to pause or to ask open-ended questions, but even here your pauses are slightly too long, your questions a little too pointed. All in all, despite your best intentions, your performance remains clumsy and erratic, the karaoke version of empathy.

Of course, a karaoke version of empathy can sometimes be better than no version at all. If you are so oblivious to other people's feelings that you alienate all those around you, a reminder to pause or to ask an open-ended question once in a while may be just the help you need. The point here is not that you should always forgo this kind of weakness fixing. The point is that you should see it for what it is: damage control, not development. And as we mentioned earlier, damage control can prevent failure, but it will never elevate you to excellence.

Some people challenge the notion that after the age of sixteen your mental network is relatively fixed. Pointing to synaptic growth in overstimulated adult rats and in adult human amputees, they imply that, with enough repetition, training does reconfigure the brain. Superficially, they are correct. Adult rats placed in an exciting rat world of mazes, tasks, and games do grow more synapses than their bored brethren in empty cages. Likewise, an adult human who has had a limb amputated does seem to undergo some mental reconfiguration as his brain attempts to restore its equilibrium. They stretch the implications of these discoveries too far, however, when they say that you should actively try to redesign your brain through training and repetition.

Although learning through repetition may result in a few new connections, it will not help you create any new superfast T1 lines. Without underlying talent, training won't create a strength. Also, repetition in an attempt to carve new connections is simply an inefficient way to learn. As John Bruer describes in *The Myth of the First Three Years,* nature has developed three ways for you to learn as an adult: Continue to strengthen your existing synaptic connections (as happens when you perfect a talent with relevant skills and knowledge), keep losing more of your extraneous connections (as also happens when you focus on your talents and allow other connections to deteriorate), or develop a few more synaptic connections. The least efficient of the three is the last because your body has to expend relatively large amounts of energy creating the biological infrastructure (blood vessels, alpha-integrin proteins, and the like) to create these new connections.

Finally, the danger of repetitive training without underlying talent is that you burn out before you net any improvement. To improve at any activity requires persistence. In order to withstand the temptation to slacken off, you need fuel. You need a way to derive energy from the process of improving so that you can keep improving. Unfortunately, when you repeatedly try to mend a broken connection, the opposite happens. It drains you of energy. No matter how well conceived the training, your movements remain jerky and disjointed. You practice and practice, but it still feels unnatural and unsatisfying. And since there is no psychic reinforcement, it is hard to gear yourself up to try again. Mending a broken connection can quickly become an alienating, thankless task.

Most organizations, with their heavy emphasis on weakness fixing, ignore how deadening it can be. And, ironically, recent advances in training techniques have only made the situation worse. Today the most advanced training techniques suggest that "learning is not an event but a process," and so emphasis is placed on the ongoing support provided to participants *after* the training class. This approach is fruitful as long as the participants possess the necessary talent. If they don't, however, this kind of training will inevitably produce the opposite reaction from the one intended. Instead of creating in them lasting improvement, it will grind them down.

Imagine an employee who struggles with thinking strategically. He is encouraged by his company to attend their state-of-the-art strategy skills training program. Then after the class is completed, someone is assigned to follow him around for a couple of months. This "coach" observes him in meetings, rates him on his strategic thinking, points out his tiny improvements, and offers suggestions for how to improve in those areas where he is still weak. All of this is intended to help, but can you imagine anything more annoying for the employee? Every day his coach reminds him of the insights he missed, the clues he failed to spot, the connections that went begging. And every day the employee becomes a little more confused, a little more frustrated, and a lot less sure of himself.

Contrast his predicament with the feeling you get when you repeatedly use your talents. Talents have not only an "I can't help it" quality to them but also an "it feels good" quality. Somehow nature has crafted you so that with your strongest connections the signals flow both ways. Your talent causes you to react in a particular way, and immediately a good feeling seems to shoot back up the T1 line. With these signals flowing smoothly back and forth, it feels as if the line is reverberating, humming. This is the feeling of using a talent.

By imbuing talents with their own built-in feedback mechanism, nature has ensured that you will keep trying to use them. In a sense, talents are nature's attempt at a perpetual motion machine. Nature causes you to react to the world in certain recurring ways, and by making those reactions feel satisfying, it pushes you to react in that way again and again, ad infinitum. Thus, while we should still be amazed by Cal Ripken's 2,216 consecutive baseball games, Bettina's twenty-one years of housekeeping, and Charles Schulz's forty years of cartooning, we can at least explain where they were getting some of their fuel.

* * *

Your talents, your strongest synaptic connections, are the most important raw material for strength building. Identify your most powerful talents, hone them with skills and knowledge, and you will be well on your way to living the strong life.

So now comes the inevitable question: If talents are vital to strength building, how can you identify yours? The irony is that since they influence every decision you make, you are already intimately familiar with your talents. Yet they are so influential, so interwoven in the fabric of your life, that the pattern of each one is hard to discern. Hiding in plain sight, they defy description. But they do leave traces. As we shall see next, to pinpoint your talents you need to change the way you look at yourself so that you can spot these traces.

II

Discover the Source
of Your Strengths

CHAPTER 3

StrengthsFinder

- **THE TRACES OF TALENT**
- **THE STRENGTHSFINDER PROFILE**

The Traces of Talent

"How can you identify your own talents?"

First, if you want to reveal your talents, monitor your *spontaneous, top-of-mind reactions* to the situations you encounter. These top-of-mind reactions provide the best trace of your talents. They reveal the location of strong mental connections.

Kathie P., a senior manager for a computer software company, gave us a dramatic example. She was bound for her company's annual sales meeting in the Dominican Republic. Squeezing into her tiny seat she glanced around her to see who was sharing the puddle jumper. Spread out in the back row was Brad, the aggressive, opinionated, and impatient CEO. In front of him was Amy, a genius at the details of software design, the best in the company. Across from her was Martin, a gregarious, charming Brit who through his network of contacts had singlehandedly turned around their flagging European operations. And then there was Gerry, the insipid head of marketing who as usual had angled his way into the seat next to Brad.

"The problems began right after takeoff," Kathie recalled. "We had just cleared the clouds when the alarm went off. I didn't even know planes had alarms, but suddenly it started braying like a donkey—*eee—aww, eee—aww*—filling the cabin with this terrible sound. The main lights went out, and the emergency lights started flashing red. As I felt the plane drop what seemed like a thousand feet in a second or two, I looked through the open cabin door and saw both pilots, necks flushed and stiff, turn to each other. I sensed immediately that neither of them had any idea what was going on.

"There was a moment of silence in the cabin—shock, I imagine—and then suddenly everyone started talking at once. Amy craned over and said, 'Kathie, can you see the dials? Can you see the dials?' Martin pulled out a tiny bottle of Smirnoff from his bag and jokingly cried out, 'At least give me one last drink!' Gerry started rocking back and forth, moaning, 'We are all going to die. We are all going to die.' Brad was immediately at the cockpit door. I still don't know how he squeezed out of those backseats, but there he was, screaming at the top of his lungs, 'What the hell do you think you guys are doing up here?'

"Me? What was I doing?" Kathie said. "Watching, I suppose, as always. The funny thing was, nothing was wrong with the plane at all. A faulty system had triggered the alarm, and then the pilots had just panicked and pushed the plane into a sharp descent."

Each of these reactions under extreme stress revealed dominant talents and to some extent helped explain each person's performance on the job. Kathie's keen observations of human nature undoubtedly contributed to her success as a manager. Amy's instinctive need for precision was the foundation for her genius at software design. Martin's ability to find the humor in every situation had presumably endeared him to his growing network of European clients. Brad's compulsion to take charge was the foundation for his leadership. Even Gerry's wailing was confirmation of his suspect backbone (this one is not a true talent since it is hard to see where and how it could be applied productively).

While this is a dramatic example of how people reveal themselves under stress, daily life offers thousands of less intense situations that also provoke revealing reactions.

Think of a recent party where you didn't know most of the guests. Who did you spend the majority of your time with, those you knew or those you didn't? If you were drawn to the strangers, you may be a natural extrovert, and your behavior may well reflect the theme "Woo," defined later as an innate need to win others over. Conversely, if you actively sought out your closest friends and hung out with them all evening, resenting the intrusions of strangers, this is a good sign that Relator—a natural desire to deepen existing relationships—is one of your leading themes.

Recall the last time that one of your employees told you he could not come to work because his child was sick. What was your first thought? If you immediately focused on the ill child, asking what was wrong and who was going to take care of her, this may be a clue that Empathy is one of your strongest themes of talent. But if your mind instinctively jumped to the question of who would fill in for the missing employee, the theme Arranger—the ability to juggle many variables at once—is probably a dominant talent.

Or how about the last time you had to make a decision when you did not have all the facts? If you relished the uncertainty, sure in your belief that any movement, even in the wrong direction, would lead to a clearer perspective, you are probably blessed with the theme Activator, defined as a bias for action in the face of ambiguity. If you stopped short, delaying action until more facts became available, a strong Analytical theme may well be the explanation. Each of these top-of-mind reactions implies distinct patterns of behavior and therefore offers clues to your talents.

While your spontaneous reactions provide the clearest trace of your talents, here are three more clues to keep in mind: yearnings, rapid learning, and satisfactions.

Yearnings reveal the presence of a talent, particularly when they are felt early in life. At ten years of age the actors Matt Damon and Ben Affleck, already close friends, would find a quiet spot in the school cafeteria and hold meetings to discuss their latest acting "projects." At thirteen Picasso was already enrolled in adult art school. At five the architect Frank Gehry made intricate models on the living room floor with wood scraps from his father's hardware store. And Mozart had written his first symphony by the time he turned twelve.

These are the eye-catching examples, but the same holds true for each of us. Perhaps because of your genes, or your early experiences, as a child you found yourself drawn to some activities and repelled by others. While your brother was chasing his friends around the backyard, you settled down to tinker with the sprinkler head, pulling it apart so that you could figure out how it worked. Your analytical mind was already making its presence known.

When your mother, as a surprise on your seventh birthday, took you to McDonald's instead of having a party at home as you had planned together, you burst into tears. Even at this tender age your disciplined mind resented surprises in your routine.

These childhood passions are caused by the various synaptic connections in your brain. The weaker connections manage little pull, and when well-intentioned mothers (or other terrible circumstances) force you down a particular path, it feels strange and makes you cry. By contrast, your strongest connections are irresistible. They exert a magnetic influence, drawing you back time and again. You feel their pull, and so you yearn.

Needless to say, social or financial pressures sometimes drown out these yearnings and prevent you from acting on them. The Booker Prize–winning novelist Penelope Fitzgerald, burdened by the demands of providing for her family without the help of her alcoholic husband, wasn't able to honor her urge to write until well into her fifties. Once released by their permanent separation, this urge proved as irrepressible as a teenager's. Over the last twenty years of her life she published twelve novels, and before her recent death at eighty, she was widely considered at the top of her game, "the best of all British novelists," according to one of her peers.

Anna Mary Robertson Moses probably holds the record for stymieing a powerful talent. Born on a farm in upstate New York, she began sketching as a young child and was so intent on incorporating every nuance of her surroundings that she mixed the juice of berries and grapes to bring color to her drawings. But her ardent sketching was soon pushed aside by the demands of the farming life, and for sixty years she didn't paint at all. Finally, at the age of seventy-eight, she retired from farming, allowed herself the luxury of letting her talent loose, and, like Penelope Fitzgerald, was quickly borne aloft by its pent-up energy. By the time of her death twenty-three years later she had painted thousands of scenes remembered from her childhood, exhibited her pictures in fifteen one-woman shows, and became known around the world as the artist Grandma Moses.

Your yearnings may not prove quite as inexorable as those of Grandma Moses, but they will exert a consistent pull. They have to. Your yearnings reflect the physical reality that some of your mental connections are simply stronger than others. So no matter how repressive the external influences prove to be, these stronger connections will keep calling out to you, demanding to be heard. If you want to discover your talents, you should pay them heed.

Of course, you can occasionally be derailed by what one might call a "misyearning," such as yearning to be in public relations because of the imagined glamour of cocktail parties and receptions or aspiring to be a manager because of a need to control. (Obviously, the best way to diagnose a misyearning is to interview an incumbent in the role and learn what the day-to-day realities of the role are really like once the blush has left the rose.) These false signals aside, your yearnings are worth following as you strive to build your strengths.

Rapid learning offers another trace of talent. Sometimes a talent doesn't signal itself through yearning. For a myriad of reasons, although the talent exists within you, you don't hear its call. Instead, comparatively late in life, something sparks the talent, and it is the speed at which you learn a new skill that provides the telltale clue to the talent's presence and power.

Unlike Picasso, his precocious contemporary, Henri Matisse didn't feel any yearning toward painting. In fact, by the time he was twenty-one he had never even picked up a brush. He was a lawyer's clerk, and most of the time a sick and depressed lawyer's clerk. One afternoon while he was recuperating in bed after another bout of flu, his mother, in search of something—anything—to lighten his spirit, put a box of paints in his hands. Almost instantly both the direction and the trajectory of his life changed. He felt a surge of energy as though released from a dark prison and seeing the light for the first time. Feverishly studying a "how-to-paint" manual, Matisse filled his days with painting and drawing. Four years later, with no schooling but his own, he was accepted into the most prestigious art school in Paris and was studying under the master Gustave Moreau.

Frederick Law Olmsted needed a similar situation to spark his talent, but as with Matisse, once revealed, his talent launched him to levels of excellence in his field at an unprecedented pace. Olmsted, a restless man with little to show for his thirty years, discovered his life's calling (what today we call landscape architecture) when he visited England in 1850. There he was struck by, in his words, the "hedges, the English hedges, hawthorn hedges, all in blossom and the mild sun beaming through the watery atmosphere." A few years later, after returning to the United States and refining his ideas, he won the most extensive landscape design competition ever held: New York's Central Park. It was his first commission.

You may have had a similar experience. You start to learn a new skill—in the context of a new job, a new challenge, or a new environment—and immediately your brain seems to light up as if a whole bank of switches were suddenly flicked to "on." The steps of this skill fly down the newly opened connections at such speed that very soon the steps disappear. Your movements lose the distinctive jerkiness of the novice and instead assume the grace of the virtuoso. You leave your classmates behind. You read ahead and try things out before the curriculum says you should. You even become unpopular with the trainer as you challenge him with new questions and insights. But you don't really care because this new skill has come to you so naturally that you can't wait to put it into practice.

Of course, not everyone has experienced eureka moments that determined the direction of their lifelong career, but whether the skill is selling, presenting, architectural drafting, giving developmental feedback to an employee, preparing legal briefs, writing business plans, cleaning hotel rooms, editing newspaper articles, or booking guests on a morning TV show, if you learned it rapidly, you should look deeper. You will be able to identify the talent or talents that made it possible.

Satisfactions provide the last clue to talent. As we described in the previous chapter, your strongest synaptic connections are designed so that when you use them, it feels good. Thus, obviously, if it feels good when you perform an activity, chances are that you are using a talent.

This seems almost too simple, much like the advice that "if it feels good, do it." Clearly, it is *not* as simple as this. For various reasons—most of them having to do with our psychological history—nature has conspired to encourage a few of our more antisocial impulses. For example, have you ever caught yourself feeling good when someone else stumbles? Have you ever felt an impulse to put someone else down in public or even to shirk responsibility and blame someone else for your failings? Many people do, no matter how ignoble it seems. Each of these behaviors involves building one's good feelings on the back of someone else's bad feelings. These are not productive behaviors and should be avoided. As we said earlier, those who are tempted to use their talents to delight in other people's failure should perhaps reexamine their values.

You are better served by tuning your antenna toward identifying those *positive* activities that seem to bring you psychological strength and satisfaction. When we interviewed the excellent performers in our study, what was most striking was the sheer range of activities or outcomes that made people happy. Initially, when we asked people what aspect of their work they enjoyed the most, we heard a common refrain: Almost all of them liked their job when they met a challenge and then overcame it. However, when we probed a little deeper, the diversity—what they actually meant by "challenge"—emerged.

Some people derived satisfaction from seeing another person achieve the kind of infinitesimal improvement most of us would miss. Some people loved bringing order to chaos. Some people reveled in playing the host at a major event. Some people delighted in cleanliness, smiling to themselves as they vacuumed themselves out of a room. Some people were idea lovers. Some people mistrusted ideas and instead thrilled to the analytical challenge of finding the "truth." Some people needed to match their own standards. Some people, whether or not they had met their own standards, felt empty if they hadn't also outperformed their peers. For some people only learning was genuinely meaningful. For some people only helping others provided meaning. Some people even got a kick out of rejection—apparently because it offered them the chance to show just how persuasive they could be.

This list could legitimately become as long as the roll call of the entire human race. We are all woven so uniquely that each of us experiences slightly different satisfactions. What we are suggesting here is that you pay close attention to the situations that seem to bring you satisfaction. If you can identify them, you are well on your way to pinpointing your talents.

How can you identify your sources of satisfaction? Well, we need to tread carefully here. Telling someone how to know if she is genuinely enjoying something can be as vacuous as telling her how to know if she is in love. On some level the only sage advice is "You either feel it or you don't."

We will take a risk however, and offer you this tip: When you are performing a particular activity, try to isolate the tense you are thinking in. If all you are thinking about is the present—"When will this be over?"—more than likely you are not using a talent. But if you find yourself thinking in the future, if you find yourself actually anticipating the activity—"When can I do this again?"—it is a pretty good sign that you are enjoying it and that one of your talents is in play.

* * *

Spontaneous reactions, yearnings, rapid learning, and satisfactions will all help you detect the traces of your talents. As you rush through your busy life, try to step back, quiet the wind whipping past your ears, and listen for these clues. They will help you zero in on your talents.

The StrengthsFinder Profile

"How does it work, and how do I complete it?"

How Does It Work?

Probably the best way to pinpoint your talents is to monitor your behavior and your feelings over an extended period of time, paying particular attention to the clues we described above. It would be hard for any profile or questionnaire to compete with this kind of focused analysis. However, as many of us do, you may struggle to find the time and the objectivity to analyze yourself in this way. You are too busy and too close to the action.

The StrengthsFinder Profile was designed to help you sharpen your perception. It presents you with pairs of statements, captures your choices, sorts them, and reflects back your most dominant patterns of behavior, thereby highlighting where you have the greatest potential for real strength.

As we just described, in the real world your spontaneous reactions to the situations you encounter help reveal your talents. For a profile to identify your talents accurately, it must mirror this process. It must give you a stimulus, offer you a selection of possible reactions, and then measure how you react. Simple.

Well, no. Building a profile to measure talent is a good deal more complicated than it appears.

The first problem is that when you react in real life, you are not presented with a set number of choices, which you then rate on a scale of 1 to 5. Rather, for every reaction there are an infinite number of choices. Your brain quickly filters these choices, and, guided by your strongest synaptic connections, it selects one. When building the StrengthsFinder Profile we couldn't give you an infinite number of choices. In fact, we planned to give you only two. To make these two choices count, we had to be sure that at least one of them reflected the presence of an underlying talent. We achieved this by asking almost two million people open-ended questions and listening to find out whether some of these questions elicited similar kinds of responses from people with similar talents.

For example, we asked managers to respond to this question: "What is the best way to motivate someone?" We weren't exactly sure what we were listening for, but to our surprise a pattern quickly emerged. Those managers with the talent to see the differences in people all answered in the same way. "It depends on the person," they said. Then we asked another question: "How closely should people be supervised?" These managers gave the same answer: "It depends on the person." This isn't the "right" answer to this question, but it does seem to reflect the presence of a distinct pattern of thinking.

Using discoveries such as this, we then crafted statements that presented "It depends on the person" as one of the choices. Those who consistently selected this choice probably possessed the talent of Individualization.

The second problem was that we couldn't make the choices too obvious. If we designed paired statements where one of the two was blatantly right and the other wrong, the choices would be skewed and would no longer accurately predict the presence or absence of a particular talent. To solve this problem we decided that most statement pairs would not be opposites. For example, when we asked millions of people "When you are talking to someone, how do you know if you are doing a good job of listening?" we found two distinct patterns of response. People with analytical talent answered like this: "I know that I am doing a good job of listening if I can understand and repeat back what the other person is saying." By contrast, people with a talent for empathy gave a very different answer: "I know that I am doing a good job of listening if the other person keeps talking."

Again, neither of these answers is "right"—in fact, on the surface both appear eminently sensible—nor are they exact opposites. However, guided by our research we now know that if we present these two statements, the choice made provides a clue as to whether the person possesses a dominant talent of empathy or analysis. It is possible, of course, for a person to have both of these talents; when faced with these two statements, the person will feel pulled equally in both directions. To accommodate this we made sure that many other opportunities would be given throughout the profile to reveal the presence of either empathy or analysis.

The last problem concerns spontaneity. In real life the decisions come so fast that you don't have time to stop, weigh all relevant options, and then select the most appropriate one. On the contrary, even when you are involved in something as simple as a conversation, your brain is making instantaneous decisions about tone, inflection, gaze, body language, words, and logic flow. To mirror the speed of real-life decision-making, we decided to impose a time limit. After each pair of statements flashes on the screen, you will have twenty seconds to respond. Twenty seconds is just enough time for you to read and comprehend both statements, but not enough time to allow your intellect to affect your choice.

What Will You Receive?

StrengthsFinder's purpose is not to anoint you with strengths but to *find where you have the greatest potential for a strength.* Thus, the StrengthsFinder Profile measures the thirty-four themes of talent that we discovered during our long study of excellence.

Once you have completed the profile you will immediately receive your five most dominant themes of talent, your signature themes. These themes of talent may not yet be strengths. Each theme is a recurring pattern of thought, feeling, or behavior—the promise of a strength. What follows is a guide to the thirty-four themes of talent. In it you will find detailed descriptions of each theme and quotes from people who possess the theme. You may not want to read all the themes and quotes in one sitting. Instead, once you have completed the StrengthsFinder Profile and received your signature themes, you can turn to the relevant pages for each of your themes and start there.

How Do You Complete the StrengthsFinder Profile?

Look on the inside of the back cover of this book and you will find a scratch-off panel, which conceals a unique personal identification code. Note the code. Now log on to the Internet and go to the following address: http://www.strengthsfinder.com. Follow the instructions and, when prompted, insert your ID code. (To complete the profile you will require a 28.8 modem or faster, and version 4.0 or higher of Internet Explorer, Netscape, or AOL.) The StrengthsFinder Profile will orient you to the system by showing you one sample pair of statements, and then the paired statements from the profile itself will begin.

As you select one of the paired statements, remember that you should respond with your top-of-mind answer. Try not to analyze your response in detail. And don't be concerned if you find yourself marking "Neutral" for some of the statements. The purpose of StrengthsFinder is to isolate your signature themes. If neither of the paired statements triggers a strong reaction or if both statements fit you equally well, then obviously this statement pair hasn't tapped into one of your most dominant themes. In either case, "Neutral" is an appropriate response.

A final word of reassurance: We have found that some people are nervous about taking the profile because they worry that their signature themes will not be "good" themes. This worry is misplaced. A theme in isolation is neither good nor bad. It is simply a recurring pattern that can either be cultivated into a strength or squandered. To be sure, when you complete the StrengthsFinder Profile your immediate reaction to your five signature themes will be affected by those very themes. For example, if you discover that Activator is one of your signature themes you will probably react by demanding to know what you can actually do with this new knowledge. If Analytical is one of your top-five, you will immediately start to wonder how we derived this theme from your responses. Your most powerful themes will always filter your world and prompt you to react in certain recurring ways. However, no matter what your themes are, try not to react by listening to that suggestive, critical little voice saying "Maybe you failed the test." You didn't. You can't fail StrengthsFinder because every signature theme contains the promise of a strength. The only possible failure would be never managing to find the right role or the right partners to help you realize that strength.

CHAPTER 4

The Thirty-four Themes of StrengthsFinder

- **ACHIEVER • ACTIVATOR • ADAPTABILITY**
- **ANALYTICAL • ARRANGER • BELIEF • COMMAND**
- **COMMUNICATION • COMPETITION**
- **CONNECTEDNESS • CONSISTENCY • CONTEXT**
- **DELIBERATIVE • DEVELOPER • DISCIPLINE • EMPATHY**
- **FOCUS • FUTURISTIC • HARMONY**
- **IDEATION • INCLUDER • INDIVIDUALIZATION**
- **INPUT • INTELLECTION • LEARNER**
- **MAXIMIZER • POSITIVITY • RELATOR**
- **RESPONSIBILITY • RESTORATIVE • SELF-ASSURANCE**
- **SIGNIFICANCE • STRATEGIC • WOO**

Note: You will notice that the theme names are not all the same "type." Some refer to the person (e.g., Achiever, Activator). Some refer to the category (e.g., Discipline, Empathy). Others refer to the quality (e.g., Adaptability, Analytical). We chose this approach because attempts to standardize the type yielded increasingly clumsy and unfamiliar terms.

ACHIEVER

Your Achiever theme helps explain your drive. Achiever describes a constant need for achievement. You feel as if every day starts at zero. By the end of the day you must achieve something tangible in order to feel good about yourself. And by "every day" you mean every single day—workdays, weekends, vacations. No matter how much you may feel you deserve a day of rest, if the day passes without some form of achievement, no matter how small, you will feel dissatisfied. You have an internal fire burning inside you. It pushes you to do more, to achieve more. After each accomplishment is reached, the fire dwindles for a moment, but very soon it rekindles itself, forcing you toward the next accomplishment. Your relentless need for achievement might not be logical. It might not even be focused. But it will always be with you. As an Achiever you must learn to live with this whisper of discontent. It does have its benefits. It brings you the energy you need to work long hours without burning out. It is the jolt you can always count on to get you started on new tasks, new challenges. It is the power supply that causes you to set the pace and define the levels of productivity for your work group. It is the theme that keeps you moving.

Achiever sounds like this:

Melanie K., ER nurse: "I have to rack up points every day to feel successful. Today I've been here only half an hour, but I've probably racked up 30 points already. I ordered equipment for the ER, I had equipment repaired, I had a meeting with my charge nurse, I brainstormed with my secretary about improving our computerized logbook. So on my list of ninety things I have thirty done already. I'm feeling pretty good about myself right now."

Ted S., salesperson: "Last year I was salesperson of the year out of my company's three hundred salespeople. It felt good for a day, but sure enough, later that week it was as if it never happened. I was back at zero again. Sometimes I wish I wasn't because it can lead me away from a balanced life toward obsession. I used to think I could change myself, but now I know I am just wired this way. This theme is truly a double-edged sword. It helps me achieve my goals, but on the other hand I wish I could just turn it off and on at will. But, hey, I can't. But I *can* manage it and avoid work obsession by focusing on achieving in all parts of my life, not just work."

Sara L., writer: "This theme is a weird one. First, it's good because you live in pursuit of the perpetual challenge. But in the second place, you never feel as though you've reached your goal. It can keep you running uphill at seventy miles an hour for your whole life. You never rest because there's always more to do. But, on balance, I think I would rather have it than not. I call it my 'divine restlessness,' and if it makes me feel as if I owe the present everything I have, then so be it. I can live with that."

ACTIVATOR

"When can we start?" This is a recurring question in your life. You are impatient for action. You may concede that analysis has its uses or that debate and discussion can occasionally yield some valuable insights, but deep down you know that only action is real. Only action can make things happen. Only action leads to performance. Once a decision is made, you cannot not act. Others may worry that "there are still some things we don't know," but this doesn't seem to slow you. If the decision has been made to go across town, you know that the fastest way to get there is to go stoplight to stoplight. You are not going to sit around waiting until all the lights have turned green. Besides, in your view, action and thinking are not opposites. In fact, guided by your Activator theme, you believe that action is the best device for learning. You make a decision, you take action, you look at the result, and you learn. This learning informs your next action and your next. How can you grow if you have nothing to react to? Well, you believe you can't. You must put yourself out there. You must take the next step. It is the only way to keep your thinking fresh and informed. The bottom line is this: You know you will be judged not by what you say, not by what you think, but by what you get done. This does not frighten you. It pleases you.

Activator sounds like this:

Jane C., Benedictine nun: "When I was prioress in the 1970s, we were hit by the energy shortage, and costs sky-rocketed. We had 140 acres, and I walked the acreage every day pondering what we should do about this energy shortage. Suddenly I decided that if we had that much land, we should be drilling our own gas well, and so we did. We spent $100,000 to drill a gas well. If you have never drilled a gas well, you probably don't realize what I didn't realize: namely, that you have to spend $70,000 just to drill to see if you have any gas on your property at all. So they dug down with some kind of vibratory camera thing, and they told me that I had a gas pool. But they didn't know how large the pool was, and they didn't know if there was enough pressure to bring it up. 'If you pay another $30,000, we will try to release the well,' they said. 'If you don't want us to, we'll just cap the well, take your $70,000, and go home.' So I gave them the final $30,000 and, fortunately, up it came. That was twenty years ago, and it is still pumping."

Jim L., entrepreneur: "Some people see my impatience as not wanting to listen to the traps, the potential roadblocks. What I keep repeating is 'I want to know when I am going to hit the wall, and I need you to tell me how much it is going to hurt. But if I choose to bump into the wall anyway, then, don't worry, you've done your job. I just had to experience it for myself.' "

ADAPTABILITY

You live in the moment. You don't see the future as a fixed destination. Instead, you see it as a place that you create out of the choices that you make right now. And so you discover your future one choice at a time. This doesn't mean that you don't have plans. You probably do. But this theme of Adaptability does enable you to respond willingly to the demands of the moment even if they pull you away from your plans. Unlike some, you don't resent sudden requests or unforeseen detours. You expect them. They are inevitable. Indeed, on some level you actually look forward to them. You are, at heart, a very flexible person who can stay productive when the demands of work are pulling you in many different directions at once.

Adaptability sounds like this:

Marie T., television producer: "I love live TV because you never know what is going to happen. One minute I might be putting together a segment on the best teenage holiday gifts, and the next I will be doing the preinterview for a presidential candidate. I guess I have always been this way. I live in the moment. If someone asks me, 'What are you doing tomorrow?' my answer is always 'Hell, I don't know. Depends what I am in the mood for.' I drive my boyfriend crazy because he'll plan for us to go to the antique market on Sunday afternoon, and then right at the last minute I'll change my mind and say, 'Nah, let's go home and read the Sunday papers.' Annoying, right? Yeah, but on the positive side, it does mean that I'm up for anything."

Linda G., project manager: "Where I work I am the calmest person I know. When someone comes in and says, 'We didn't plan right. We need this turned around by tomorrow,' my colleagues seem to tense up and freeze. Somehow that doesn't happen to me. I like that pressure, that need for instant response. It makes me feel alive."

Peter F., corporate trainer: "I think I deal with life better than most people. Last week I found that my car window had been smashed and the stereo stolen. I was annoyed, of course, but it didn't throw me off my day one bit. I just cleared it, mentally moved on, and went right on with the other things I had to get done that day."

ANALYTICAL

Your Analytical theme challenges other people: "Prove it. Show me why what you are claiming is true." In the face of this kind of questioning some will find that their brilliant theories wither and die. For you, this is precisely the point. You do not necessarily want to destroy other people's ideas, but you do insist that their theories be sound. You see yourself as objective and dispassionate. You like data because they are value free. They have no agenda. Armed with these data, you search for patterns and connections. You want to understand how certain patterns affect one another. How do they combine? What is their outcome? Does this outcome fit with the theory being offered or the situation being confronted? These are your questions. You peel the layers back until, gradually, the root cause or causes are revealed. Others see you as logical and rigorous. Over time they will come to you in order to expose someone's "wishful thinking" or "clumsy thinking" to your refining mind. It is hoped that your analysis is never delivered too harshly. Otherwise, others may avoid you when that "wishful thinking" is their own.

Analytical sounds like this:

Jose G., school system administrator: "I have an innate ability to see structures and formats and patterns before they exist. For instance, when people are talking about writing a grant proposal, while I'm listening to them my brain instinctively processes the type of grants that are available and how the discussion fits into the eligibility, right down to the format of how the information can fit on the grant form in a clear and convincing way."

Jack T., human resources executive: "If I make a claim, I need to know that I can back it up with facts and logical thinking. For example, if someone says that our company is not paying as much as other companies, I always ask, 'Why do you say that?' If they say, 'Well, I saw an ad in the paper that offers graduates in mechanical engineering five grand more than we are paying,' I'll reply by asking, 'But where are these graduates going to work? Is their salary based on geography? What types of companies are they going for? Are they manufacturing companies like ours? And how many people are in their sample? Is it three people, and one of them got a really good deal, thus driving the overall average up?' There are many questions I need to ask to ensure that their claim is indeed a fact and not based on one misleading data point."

Leslie J., school principal: "Many times there are inconsistencies in the performance of the same group of students from one year to the next. It's the same group of kids, but their scores are different year to year. How can this be? Which building are the kids in? How many of the kids have been enrolled for a full academic year? Which teachers were they assigned to, and what teaching styles were used by those teachers? I just love asking questions like these to understand what is truly happening."

ARRANGER

You are a conductor. When faced with a complex situation involving many factors, you enjoy managing all of the variables, aligning and realigning them until you are sure you have arranged them in the most productive configuration possible. In your mind there is nothing special about what you are doing. You are simply trying to figure out the best way to get things done. But others, lacking this theme, will be in awe of your ability. "How can you keep so many things in your head at once?" they will ask. "How can you stay so flexible, so willing to shelve well-laid plans in favor of some brand-new configuration that has just occurred to you?" But you cannot imagine behaving in any other way. You are a shining example of effective flexibility, whether you are changing travel schedules at the last minute because a better fare has popped up or mulling over just the right combination of people and resources to accomplish a new project. From the mundane to the complex, you are always looking for the perfect configuration. Of course, you are at your best in dynamic situations. Confronted with the unexpected, some complain that plans devised with such care cannot be changed, while others take refuge in the existing rules or procedures. You don't do either. Instead, you jump into the confusion, devising new options, hunting for new paths of least resistance, and figuring out new partnerships—because, after all, there might just be a better way.

Arranger sounds like this:

Sarah P., finance executive: "I love really complicated challenges where I have to think on my feet and figure out how all the pieces fit together. Some people look at a situation, see thirty variables, and get hung up trying to balance all thirty. When I look at the same situation, I see about three options. And because I see only three, it's easier for me to make a decision and then put everything into place."

Grant D., operations manager: "I got a message the other day from our manufacturing facility saying that demand for one of our products had greatly exceeded the forecast. I thought about it for a moment, and then an idea popped into my head: Ship the product weekly, not monthly. So I said, 'Let's contact our European subsidiaries, ask them what their demand is, tell them the situation we are in, and then ask what their weekly demand is.' That way we can meet requirements without building up our inventory. Sure, it'll drive shipping costs up, but that's better than having too much inventory in one place and not enough in another."

Jane B., entrepreneur: "Sometimes, for instance, when we are all going to a movie or a football game, this Arranger theme drives me up the wall. My family and friends come to rely on me—'Jane will get the tickets, Jane will organize the transportation.' Why should I always have to do it? But they just say, 'Because you do it well. For us it would take half an hour. For you it seems to go much faster. You just call up the ticket place, order the right tickets, and just like that it's done.' "

BELIEF

If you possess a strong Belief theme, you have certain core values that are enduring. These values vary from one person to another, but ordinarily your Belief theme causes you to be family-oriented, altruistic, even spiritual, and to value responsibility and high ethics—both in yourself and others. These core values affect your behavior in many ways. They give your life meaning and satisfaction; in your view, success is more than money and prestige. They provide you with direction, guiding you through the temptations and distractions of life toward a consistent set of priorities. This consistency is the foundation for all your relationships. Your friends call you dependable. "I know where you stand," they say. Your Belief makes you easy to trust. It also demands that you find work that meshes with your values. Your work must be meaningful, it must matter to you. And guided by your Belief theme it will matter only if it gives you a chance to live out your values.

Belief sounds like this:

Michael K., salesperson: "The vast majority of my non-working time goes to my family and to the things we do in the community. I was on the countywide Boy Scouts board of directors. And when I was a Boy Scout, I was pack leader. When I was an Explorer, I was junior assistant leader for the Boy Scouts. I just like being with kids. I believe that's where the future is.

And I think you can do a whole lot worse with your time than investing it in the future."

Lara M., college president: "My values are why I work so hard every day at my job. I put hours and hours into this job, and I don't even care what I get paid. I just found out that I am the lowest paid college president in my state, and I don't even care. I mean, I don't do this for the money."

Tracy D., airline executive: "If you are not doing something important, why bother? Getting up every day and working on ways to make flying safer seems important to me, purposeful. If I didn't find this purpose in my job, I don't know if I could work through all the challenges and frustrations that get in my way. I think I would get demoralized."

COMMAND

Command leads you to take charge. Unlike some people, you feel no discomfort with imposing your views on others. On the contrary, once your opinion is formed, you *need* to share it with others. Once your goal is set, you feel restless until you have aligned others with you. You are not frightened by confrontation; rather, you know that confrontation is the first step toward resolution. Whereas others may avoid facing up to life's unpleasantness, you feel compelled to present the facts or the truth, no matter how unpleasant it may be. You need things to be clear between people and challenge them to be clear-eyed and honest. You push them to take risks. You may even intimidate them. And while some may resent this, labeling you opinionated, they often willingly hand you the reins. People are drawn toward those who take a stance and ask them to move in a certain direction. Therefore, people will be drawn to you. You have presence. You have Command.

Command sounds like this:

Malcolm M., hospitality manager: "One reason I affect people is that I am so candid. Actually, people say that I intimidate them at first. After I work with them a year, we talk about that sometimes. They say, 'Boy, Malcolm, when I started working here, I was scared to death.' When I ask why, they say, 'I've never worked with anyone who just said it. Whatever it was, whatever needed to be said, you just said it.' "

Rick P., retail executive: "We have a wellness program whereby if you consume less than four alcoholic beverages a week, you get $25; if you don't smoke, you get $25 a month. So one day I got word that one of my store managers was smoking again. This was not good. He was smoking in the store, setting a bad example to the employees, and claiming his $25. I just can't keep stuff like that inside. It wasn't comfortable, but I confronted him with it immediately and clearly. 'Stop doing that, or you are fired.' He's basically a good guy, but you can't let things like that slide by."

Diane N., hospice worker: "I don't think of myself as assertive, but I do take charge. When you walk into a room with a dying person and his family, you have to take charge. They want you to take charge. They are a bit in shock, a bit frightened, a bit in denial. Basically, they're confused. They need someone to tell them what is going to happen next, what they can expect; that it's not going to be fun but that in some important ways it will be all right. They don't want mousy and soft. They want clarity and honesty. I provide it."

COMMUNICATION

You like to explain, to describe, to host, to speak in public, and to write. This is your Communication theme at work. Ideas are a dry beginning. Events are static. You feel a need to bring them to life, to energize them, to make them exciting and vivid. And so you turn events into stories and practice telling them. You take the dry idea and enliven it with images and examples and metaphors. You believe that most people have a very short attention span. They are bombarded by information, but very little of it survives. You want your information—whether an idea, an event, a product's features and benefits, a discovery, or a lesson—to survive. You want to divert their attention toward you and then capture it, lock it in. This is what drives your hunt for the perfect phrase. This is what draws you toward dramatic words and powerful word combinations. This is why people like to listen to you. Your word pictures pique their interest, sharpen their world, and inspire them to act.

Communication sounds like this:

Sheila K., general manager of a theme park: "Stories are the best way to make my point. Yesterday I wanted to show my executive committee the impact we can have on our guests, so I shared this story with them: One of our employees brought her father to the flag-raising ceremony we have for Veterans Day here at the theme park. He was disabled during World War II, and he now has a rare form of cancer and has had a lot of surgery. He's dying. At the start of the little ceremony one of our employees said to the group, 'This man is a World War II veteran. Can we give him a hand?' Everybody cheered, and his daughter started crying. Her dad took off his hat. He never takes off his hat because of the scars on his head from the war and the cancer surgery, but when the national anthem started, he took off his hat and bowed his head. His daughter told me later that it was the best day he's had in years."

Tom P., banking executive: "My most recent client thought that the flow of capital toward Internet stocks was just a passing phase. I tried using rational argument to change his mind, but he couldn't or wouldn't be convinced. In the end, as I often do when faced with a client in denial, I resorted to imagery. I told him that he was like a person sitting on a beach with his back to the sea. The Internet was like a fast-rising tide. No matter how comfortable he felt right now, the tide was rising with each crashing wave, and very soon one of those waves would come crashing down over his head and engulf him. He got the point."

Margret D., marketing director: "I once read a book about giving speeches that gave two suggestions: talk only about things you're really passionate about and always use personal examples. I immediately started doing that, and I found lots of stories because I have kids and grandkids and a husband. I build my stories around my personal experiences because everyone can relate to them."

COMPETITION

Competition is rooted in comparison. When you look at the world, you are instinctively aware of other people's performance. Their performance is the ultimate yardstick. No matter how hard you tried, no matter how worthy your intentions, if you reached your goal but did not outperform your peers, the achievement feels hollow. Like all competitors, you need other people. You need to compare. If you can compare, you can compete, and if you can compete, you can win. And when you win, there is no feeling quite like it. You like measurement because it facilitates comparisons. You like other competitors because they invigorate you. You like contests because they must produce a winner. You particularly like contests where you know you have the inside track to be the winner. Although you are gracious to your fellow competitors and even stoic in defeat, you don't compete for the fun of competing. You compete to win. Over time you will come to avoid contests where winning seems unlikely.

Competition sounds like this:

Mark L., sales executive: "I've played sports my entire life, and I don't just play to have fun, let me put it that way. I like to engage in sports I am going to win and not ones I am going to lose because if I lose, I am outwardly gracious but inwardly infuriated."

Harry D., general manager: "I'm not a big sailor, but I love the America's Cup. Both boats are supposed to be exactly the same, and both crews are top-notch athletes. But you always get a winner. One of them had some secret up their sleeve that tipped the balance and enabled them to win more often than lose. And that's what I am looking for—that secret, that tiny edge."

Sumner Redstone, chairman of Viacom Corporation, on his acquisition of the television network CBS: "For me being number one was always a big thing. What I saw was that we'd have the number one cable network! The number one broadcast network! The number one outdoor-advertising company! The number one TV programming! Across the board—number ones!"

CONNECTEDNESS

Things happen for a reason. You are sure of it. You are sure of it because in your soul you know that we are all connected. Yes, we are individuals, responsible for our own judgments and in possession of our own free will, but nonetheless we are part of something larger. Some may call it the collective unconscious. Others may label it spirit or life force. But whatever your word of choice, you gain confidence from knowing that we are not isolated from one another or from the earth and the life on it. This feeling of Connectedness implies certain responsibilities. If we are all part of a larger picture, then we must not harm others because we will be harming ourselves. We must not exploit because we will be exploiting ourselves. Your awareness of these responsibilities creates your value system. You are considerate, caring, and accepting. Certain of the unity of humankind, you are a bridge builder for people of different cultures. Sensitive to the invisible hand, you can give others comfort that there is a purpose beyond our humdrum lives. The exact articles of your faith will depend on your upbringing and your culture, but your faith is strong. It sustains you and your close friends in the face of life's mysteries.

Connectedness sounds like this:

Mandy M., homemaker: "Humility is the essence of Connectedness. You have to know who you are and who you aren't. I have a piece of the wisdom. I don't have much of it, but what I do have is real. This isn't grandiosity. This is real humility. You have confidence in your gifts, real confidence, but you know you don't have all the answers. You start to feel connected to others because you know they have wisdom that you don't. You can't feel connected if you think you have everything."

Rose T., psychologist: "Sometimes I just look at my bowl of cereal in the morning and think about those hundreds of people who were involved in bringing me my bowl of cereal: the farmers in the field; the biochemists who made the pesticides; the warehouse workers at the food preparation plants; even the marketers who somehow persuaded me to buy this box of cereal and not a different one sitting next to it on a shelf. I know it sounds strange, but I give thanks to these people, and just doing that makes me feel more involved with life, more connected to things, less alone."

Chuck M., teacher: "In life I tend to be very black and white about things, but when it comes to understanding the mysteries of life, for some reason I am much more open. I have a big interest in learning about all different religions. I am reading a book right now that talks about Judaism versus Christianity versus the religion of the Canaanites. Buddhism, Greek mythology, it's really interesting how all of these tie together in some way."

CONSISTENCY

Balance is important to you. You are keenly aware of the need to treat people the same, no matter what their station in life, so you do not want to see the scales tipped too far in any one person's favor. In your view this leads to selfishness and individualism. It leads to a world where some people gain an unfair advantage because of their connections or their background or their greasing of the wheels. This is truly offensive to you. You see yourself as a guardian against it. In direct contrast to this world of special favors, you believe that people function best in a consistent environment where the rules are clear and are applied to everyone equally. This is an environment where people know what is expected. It is predictable and evenhanded. It is fair. Here each person has an even chance to show his or her worth.

Consistency sounds like this:

Simon H., general manager of a hotel: "I often remind my senior managers that they shouldn't be abusing their parking privileges or using their position to take golf tee times when there are guests waiting. They hate my drawing attention to this, but I am just the kind of person who dislikes people abusing their perks. I also spend a great deal of time with our hourly employees. I have tremendous respect for them. In fact, as I told my managers, the lower people are on the totem pole, the better I treat them."

Jamie K., magazine editor: "I am the person who always roots for the underdog. I hate it when people don't get a fair shot because of some circumstance in their life that they couldn't control. To put some teeth to this, I am going to set up a scholarship at my alma mater so that journalism students of limited means can do internships in the real world without having to keep paying for their college tuition. I was lucky. When I was an intern in New York at NBC, my family could afford it. Some families can't, but those students should still get a fair shot."

Ben F., operations manager: "Always give credit where credit is due, that's my motto. If I am in a meeting and I bring up an idea that one of my staff actually came up with, I make sure to publicly attribute the idea to that person. Why? Because my bosses always did that with me, and now it seems like the only fair and proper thing to do."

CONTEXT

You look back. You look back because that is where the answers lie. You look back to understand the present. From your vantage point the present is unstable, a confusing clamor of competing voices. It is only by casting your mind back to an earlier time, a time when the plans were being drawn up, that the present regains its stability. The earlier time was a simpler time. It was a time of blueprints. As you look back, you begin to see these blueprints emerge. You realize what the initial intentions were. These blueprints or intentions have since become so embellished that they are almost unrecognizable, but now this Context theme reveals them again. This understanding brings you confidence. No longer disoriented, you make better decisions because you sense the underlying structure. You become a better partner because you understand how your colleagues came to be who they are. And counterintuitively you become wiser about the future because you saw its seeds being sown in the past. Faced with new people and new situations, it will take you a little time to orient yourself, but you must give yourself this time. You must discipline yourself to ask the questions and allow the blueprints to emerge because no matter what the situation, if you haven't seen the blueprints, you will have less confidence in your decisions.

Context sounds like this:

Adam Y., software designer: "I tell my people, 'Let's avoid *vuja de*.' And they say, 'Isn't that the wrong word? Shouldn't it be *déjà vu*?' And I say, 'No, *vuja de* means that we're bound to repeat the mistakes of our past. We must avoid this. We must look to our past, see what led to our mistakes, and then not make them again.' It sounds obvious, but most people don't look to their past or don't trust that it was valid or something. And so for them its *vuja de* all over again."

Jesse K., media analyst: "I have very little empathy, so I don't relate to people through their present emotional state.

Instead, I relate to them through their past. In fact, I can't even begin to understand people until I have found out where they grew up, who their parents were, what they studied at college."

Gregg H., accounting manager: "I recently moved the whole office to a new accounting system, and the only reason it worked was that I honored their past. When people build an accounting system, it's their blood, their sweat and tears, it's them. They are personally identified with it. So if I come in and blandly tell them that I'm going to change it, it's like me saying I am going to take your baby away. That's the level of emotion I was dealing with. I had to respect this connection, this history, or they would have rejected me out of hand."

DELIBERATIVE

You are careful. You are vigilant. You are a private person. You know that the world is an unpredictable place. Everything may seem in order, but beneath the surface you sense the many risks. Rather than denying these risks, you draw each one out into the open. Then each risk can be identified, assessed, and ultimately reduced. Thus, you are a fairly serious person who approaches life with a certain reserve. For example, you like to plan ahead so as to anticipate what might go wrong. You select your friends cautiously and keep your own counsel when the conversation turns to personal matters. You are careful not to give too much praise and recognition, lest it be misconstrued. If some people don't like you because you are not as effusive as others, then so be it. For you, life is not a popularity contest. Life is something of a minefield. Others can run through it recklessly if they so choose, but you take a different approach. You identify the dangers, weigh their relative impact, and then place your feet deliberately. You walk with care.

Deliberative sounds like this:

Dick H., film producer: "My whole thing is to reduce the number of variables out there. The fewer the variables, the lower the risk. When I am negotiating with directors, I always start by giving in on some of the smaller points right away. Then once I have taken the smaller issues out of play, I feel better. I can focus. I can control the conversation."

Debbie M., project manager: "I am the practical one. When my colleagues are spouting all of these wonderful ideas, I am asking questions like 'How is this going to work?' 'How is this going to be accepted by this group or that group of people?' I won't say that I play devil's advocate because that is too negative, but I do weigh the implications and assess risk. And I think we all make better decisions because of my questions."

Jamie B., service worker: "I am not a very organized person, but the one thing I do without fail is double-check. I don't do it because I am hyperresponsible or anything. I do it to feel secure. With relationships, with performance, with anything, I am out there on a limb, and I need to know that the particular branch I am standing on is solid."

Brian B., school administrator: "I am putting together a safe schools plan. I am going to conferences, and we have eight committees working. We have a districtwide review board, but I am still not comfortable with the basic model. My boss asks, 'When can I see the plan?' And I say, 'Not yet. I am not comfortable.' She has a big smile on her face and says, 'Gee, Brian, I don't want it to be perfect, I just want a plan.' But she lets me be because she knows that the care I take now pays big dividends. Because of this pre-work, once the decision is made, it stays made. It doesn't unravel."

DEVELOPER

You see the potential in others. Very often, in fact, potential is all you see. In your view no individual is fully formed. On the contrary, each individual is a work in progress, alive with possibilities. And you are drawn toward people for this very reason. When you interact with others, your goal is to help them experience success. You look for ways to challenge them. You devise interesting experiences that can stretch them and help them grow. And all the while you are on the lookout for the signs of growth—a new behavior learned or modified, a slight improvement in a skill, a glimpse of excellence or of "flow" where previously there were only halting steps. For you these small increments—invisible to some—are clear signs of potential being realized. These signs of growth in others are your fuel. They bring you strength and satisfaction. Over time many will seek you out for help and encouragement because on some level they know that your helpfulness is both genuine and fulfilling to you.

Developer sounds like this:

Marilyn K., college president: "When it's graduation time and a nursing student walks across the stage, it's usually a woman around thirty-five. She gets her diploma, and about eighteen rows back some little kid is standing on a chair with a group yelling, 'Yeah, Mom!' I love that. I cry every time."

John M., advertising executive: "I'm not a lawyer, doctor, or candlestick maker. My skills are of a different type. They have to do with understanding people and motives, and the pleasure I get is from watching people discover themselves in ways they never thought possible and from finding people who bring talents to the table that I don't have."

Anna G., nurse: "I had a patient, a young woman, with lung damage so bad that she will have to be on oxygen forever. She will never have the energy or the strength to live a normal life, and I walk in and she's desperate. She doesn't know if she is short of breath because she is anxious, or anxious because she is short of breath. And she's talking suicide because she can't work, can't support her husband. So I got her thinking about what she could do rather than what she couldn't. It turns out that she is very creative with arts and crafts, so I told her, 'Look, there are things you can do, and if those things bring you pleasure, then do them. It's a place to start.' And she cried and said, 'I have the energy to wash only one bowl.' I said, 'That's today. Tomorrow you can wash two.' And by Christmas time she was making all kinds of things and selling them, too."

DISCIPLINE

Your world needs to be predictable. It needs to be ordered and planned. So you instinctively impose structure on your world. You set up routines. You focus on timelines and deadlines. You break long-term projects into a series of specific short-term plans, and you work through each plan diligently. You are not necessarily neat and clean, but you do need precision. Faced with the inherent messiness of life, you want to feel in control. The routines, the timelines, the structure, all of these help create this feeling of control. Lacking this theme of Discipline, others may sometimes resent your need for order, but there need not be conflict. You must understand that not everyone feels your urge for predictability; they have other ways of getting things done. Likewise, you can help them understand and even appreciate your need for structure. Your dislike of surprises, your impatience with errors, your routines, and your detail orientation don't need to be misinterpreted as controlling behaviors that box people in. Rather, these behaviors can be understood as your instinctive method for maintaining your progress and your productivity in the face of life's many distractions.

Discipline sounds like this:

Les T., hospitality manager: "The turning point in my career was attending one of those time-management courses some years back. I was always disciplined, but the power grew when I learned how to use that discipline in an organized process every day. This little Palm Pilot means that I call my mom every Sunday rather than letting months go by without calling. It means I take my wife out for dinner every week without her asking. It means that my employees know that if I say I need to see something on Monday, I will be calling on Monday if I haven't seen it. This Palm Pilot is so much a part of my life that I have lengthened all of my pants' pockets so that it fits right there on my hip."

Troy T., sales executive: "My filing system may not look that pretty, but it is very efficient. I handwrite everything because I know that no customer is going to see these files, so why waste time making them look pretty? My whole life as a salesperson is based on deadlines and follow-up. In my system I keep track of everything so that I take responsibility not only for my deadlines and follow-up but for all of my customers' and colleagues' as well. If they haven't gotten back to me by the time they promised, they're going to receive an e-mail from me. In fact, I heard from one the other day who said, 'I may as well get back to you because I know you're going to voice-mail me if you haven't heard from me.' "

Diedre S., office manager: "I hate wasting time, so I make lists, long lists that keep me on track. Today my list has ninety items on it, and I will get through 95 percent of them. And that's discipline because I don't let anybody waste my time. I am not rude, but I can let you know in a very tactful, humorous way that your time is up."

EMPATHY

You can sense the emotions of those around you. You can feel what they are feeling as though their feelings are your own. Intuitively, you are able to see the world through their eyes and share their perspective. You do not necessarily agree with each person's perspective. You do not necessarily feel pity for each person's predicament—this would be sympathy, not empathy. You do not necessarily condone the choices each person makes, but you do understand. This instinctive ability to understand is powerful. You hear the unvoiced questions. You anticipate the need. Where others grapple for words, you seem to find the right words and the right tone. You help people find the right phrases to express their feelings—to themselves as well as to others. You help them give voice to their emotional life. For all these reasons other people are drawn to you.

Empathy sounds like this:

Alyce J., administrator: "Recently, I was in a meeting of trustees where one of the individuals was presenting a new idea that was critical to her and to the life of this group. When she was finished, no one heard her opinion, no one really heard her. It was a powerfully demoralizing moment for her. I could see it in her face, and she wasn't herself for a day or two afterward. I finally raised the issue with her and used words that helped describe how she was feeling. I said, 'Something's wrong,' and she started to talk. I said, 'I really understand. I know how important this was for you, and you don't seem like yourself,' and so on. And she finally gave words to what was going on inside her. She said, 'You're the only one who heard me and who has said one word to me about it.' "

Brian H., administrator: "When my team is making decisions, what I like to do is say, 'Okay, what will this person say about this?' 'What will that person say about it?' In other words, put yourself in their position. Let's think about the arguments from their perspective so that we can all be more persuasive."

Janet P., schoolteacher: "I never played basketball because they didn't have it for women when I was a kid, but I believe I can tell at a basketball game when the momentum is changing, and I want to go to the coach and say, 'Get them revved up. You are losing them.' Empathy also works in large groups; you can feel the crowd."

FOCUS

"Where am I headed?" you ask yourself. You ask this question every day. Guided by this theme of Focus, you need a clear destination. Lacking one, your life and your work can quickly become frustrating. And so each year, each month, and even each week you set goals. These goals then serve as your compass, helping you determine priorities and make the necessary corrections to get back on course. Your Focus is powerful because it forces you to filter; you instinctively evaluate whether or not a particular action will help you move toward your goal. Those that don't are ignored. In the end, then, your Focus forces you to be efficient. Naturally, the flip side of this is that it causes you to become impatient with delays, obstacles, and even tangents, no matter how intriguing they appear to be. This makes you an extremely valuable team member. When others start to wander down other avenues, you bring them back to the main road. Your Focus reminds everyone that if something is not helping you move toward your destination, then it is not important. And if it is not important, then it is not worth your time. You keep everyone on point.

Focus sounds like this:

Nick H., computer executive: "It is very important to me to be efficient. I'm the sort of guy who plays a round of golf in two and a half hours. When I was at Electronic Data Systems, I worked out a set list of questions so that I could conduct a review of each division in fifteen minutes. The founder, Ross Perot, called me 'The Dentist' because I would schedule a whole day of these in-and-out, fifteen-minute meetings."

Brad F., sales executive: "I am always sorting priorities, trying to figure out the most efficient route toward the goal so that there is very little dead time, very little wasted motion. For example, I will get multiple calls from customers who need me to call the service department for them, and rather than taking each one of these calls as they come and interrupting the priorities of the day, I group them together into one call at the end of the day and get it done."

Mike L., administrator: "People are amazed how I put

things into perspective and stay on track. When people around the district are stuck on issues and caught on contrived barriers, I am able to pole-vault over them, reestablish the focus, and keep things moving."

Doriane L., homemaker: "I am just the kind of person who likes to get to the point—in conversations, at work, and even when I am shopping with my husband. He likes to try on lots of things and has a good time doing it, whereas I try one thing on, and if I like it and it is not horribly priced, I buy it. I'm a surgical shopper."

FUTURISTIC

"Wouldn't it be great if . . ." You are the kind of person who loves to peer over the horizon. The future fascinates you. As if it were projected on the wall, you see in detail what the future might hold, and this detailed picture keeps pulling you forward, into tomorrow. While the exact content of the picture will depend on your other strengths and interests—a better product, a better team, a better life, or a better world—it will always be inspirational to you. You are a dreamer who sees visions of what could be and who cherishes those visions. When the present proves too frustrating and the people around you too pragmatic, you conjure up your visions of the future and they energize you. They can energize others, too. In fact, very often people look to you to describe your visions of the future. They want a picture that can raise their sights and thereby their spirits. You can paint it for them. Practice. Choose your words carefully. Make the picture as vivid as possible. People will want to latch on to the hope you bring.

Futuristic sounds like this:

Dan F., school administrator: "In any situation I am the guy who says 'Did you ever think about . . . ? I wonder if we could . . . I don't believe it can't be done. It's just that nobody has done it yet . . . Let's figure out how we can.' I am always look-ing for options, for ways not to be mired by the status quo. In fact, there is no such thing as the status quo. You are either moving forward, or you are moving backward. That's the real-ity of life, at least from my perspective. And right now I believe that my profession is moving backward. State schools are being out-serviced by private schools, charter schools, home schools, Internet schools. We need to free ourselves from our traditions and create a new future."

Dr. Jan K., internist: "Here at the Mayo Clinic we are launching a group called the Hospitalists. Rather than having patients handed off from one doctor to another during their stay in the hospital, I envision a family of providers. I envision fifteen to twenty MDs, of various genders and races, with twenty to twenty-five nurse practitioners. There will be four to five new hospital services, most of which will work with surgeons and will provide paraoperative care as well as care for the hospital-ized elderly. We are redefining the model of care here. We don't just take care of the patients when they are in the hospital. If a patient comes in for a knee replacement, a member of the Hospitalist team would see him before the surgery, follow him from the day of surgery through the days of hospitalization, and then see him when he comes in six weeks later for his postop-erative check. We will provide patients with a complete episode of care so that they don't get lost in the handoffs. And to get the funding I just saw the detailed picture in my head and kept describing this picture to the department chair. I guess I made it seem so real that they had no choice but to grant me the funds."

HARMONY

You look for areas of agreement. In your view there is little to be gained from conflict and friction, so you seek to hold them to a minimum. When you know that the people around you hold dif-fering views, you try to find the common ground. You try to steer them away from confrontation and toward harmony. In fact, harmony is one of your guiding values. You can't quite believe how much time is wasted by people trying to impose their views on others. Wouldn't we all be more productive if we kept our opinions in check and instead looked for consensus and support? You believe we would, and you live by that belief. When others are sounding off about their goals, their claims, and their fervently held opinions, you hold your peace. When others strike out in a direction, you will willingly, in the service of harmony, modify your own objectives to merge with theirs (as long as their basic values do not clash with yours). When others start to argue about their pet theory or concept, you steer clear of the debate, preferring to talk about practical, down-to-earth matters on which you can all agree. In your view we are all in the same boat, and we need this boat to get where we are going. It is a good boat. There is no need to rock it just to show that you can.

Harmony sounds like this:

Jane C., Benedictine nun: "I like people. I relate to them easily because I am very strong in adjustment. I take the shape of the vessel into which I am poured, so I don't irritate easily."

Chuck M., teacher: "I don't like conflict in class, but I have learned to let things run their course instead of trying to stop it right away. When I first started teaching, if someone said something negative, I would think, 'Oh, why did you have to say that?' and try to get rid of it right away. But now I simply try to get the opinion of someone else in the class so that perhaps we can have different points of view on the same topic."

Tom P., technician: "I can remember vividly when I was ten or eleven and some of the kids in my school would get into arguments. For some reason I would feel compelled to get in the middle of things and find the common ground. I was the peacemaker."

IDEATION

You are fascinated by ideas. What is an idea? An idea is a concept, the best explanation of the most events. You are delighted when you discover beneath the complex surface an elegantly simple concept to explain why things are the way they are. An idea is a connection. Yours is the kind of mind that is always looking for connections, and so you are intrigued when seemingly disparate phenomena can be linked by an obscure connection. An idea is a new perspective on familiar challenges. You revel in taking the world we all know and turning it around so we can view it from a strange but strangely enlightening angle. You love all these ideas because they are profound, because they are novel, because they are clarifying, because they are contrary, because they are bizarre. For all these reasons you derive a jolt of energy whenever a new idea occurs to you. Others may label you creative or original or conceptual or even smart. Perhaps you are all of these. Who can be sure? What you are sure of is that ideas are thrilling. And on most days this is enough.

Ideation sounds like this:

Mark B., writer: "My mind works by finding connections between things. The other day I was hunting down the Mona Lisa in the Louvre museum. I turned a corner and was blinded by the flashing of a thousand cameras snapping the tiny picture. For some reason I stored that visual image away. Then I noticed a NO FLASH PHOTOGRAPHY sign, and I stored that away, too. I thought it was odd because I remembered reading that flash photography can harm paintings. Then about six months later I read that the Mona Lisa has been stolen at least twice in this century. And suddenly I put it all together. The only explanation for all these facts is that the real Mona Lisa is not on display in the Louvre. The real Mona Lisa has been stolen, and the museum, afraid to admit their carelessness, has installed a fake. I don't know if it's true, of course, but what a great story."

Andrea H., interior designer: "I have the kind of mind where everything has to fit together or I start to feel very odd. For me, every piece of furniture represents an idea. It serves a discrete function both independently and in concert with every other piece. The 'idea' of each piece is so powerful in my mind, it *must* be obeyed. If I am sitting in a room where the chairs are somehow not fulfilling their discrete function—they're the wrong kind of chairs or they're facing the wrong way or they're pushed up too close to the coffee table—I find myself getting physically uncomfortable and mentally distracted. Later, I won't be able to get it out of my mind. I'll find myself awake at 3:00 A.M., and I walk through the person's house in my mind's eye, rearranging the furniture and repainting the walls. This started happening when I was very young, say seven years old."

INCLUDER

"Stretch the circle wider." This is the philosophy around which you orient your life. You want to include people and make them feel part of the group. In direct contrast to those who are drawn only to exclusive groups, you actively avoid those groups that exclude others. You want to expand the group so that as many people as possible can benefit from its support. You hate the sight of someone on the outside looking in. You want to draw them in so that they can feel the warmth of the group. You are an instinctively accepting person. Regardless of race or sex or nationality or personality or faith, you cast few judgments. Judgments can hurt a person's feelings. Why do that if you don't have to? Your accepting nature does not necessarily rest on a belief that each of us is different and that one should respect these differences. Rather, it rests on your conviction that fundamentally we are all the same. We are all equally important. Thus, no one should be ignored. Each of us should be included. It is the least we all deserve.

Includer sounds like this:

Harry B., outplacement consultant: "Even as a child, although I was very shy, I always made sure that I was the one inviting others to play. When picking teams or sides in school, I never wanted anyone not to participate with us. In fact, I can remember when I was ten or eleven, I had a friend who was not a member of our church—he was a Catholic. We were at a church banquet, and he showed up at the door because typically we had our youth activity on that night. Immediately, I got up, brought him over to our family, and sat him down at the table."

Jeremy B., defense lawyer: "When I first started this job, I met people and became fast, furious friends with them almost on day one, only to find out later that, you know, this person's got a lot of issues, and I've already included them in dinner parties and our social circle. My partner, Mark, is like 'What is it exactly that made you want to include this person?' And then it's a matter of figuring out what pushed my buttons when I first met them, that made me enjoy them so much. And, you know, making sure that this is the aspect of them that Mark and I focus on . . . because once I include someone in my circle, I don't, you know, dump them."

Giles D., corporate trainer: "In class I seem to be able to sense when someone is disengaging from the group discussion, and I immediately draw them back into the conversation. Last week we got into a lengthy discussion about performance appraisals, and one woman wasn't talking at all. So I just said, 'Monica, you've had performance appraisals. Any thoughts on the subject?' I really think this has helped me as a teacher because when I don't know the answer to something, very often it is the person I pull in who supplies the answer for me."

INDIVIDUALIZATION

Your Individualization theme leads you to be intrigued by the unique qualities of each person. You are impatient with generalizations or "types" because you don't want to obscure what is special and distinct about each person. Instead, you focus on the differences between individuals. You instinctively observe each person's style, each person's motivation, how each thinks, and how each builds relationships. You hear the one-of-a-kind stories in each person's life. This theme explains why you pick your friends just the right birthday gift, why you know that one person prefers praise in public and another detests it, and why you tailor your teaching style to accommodate one person's need to be shown and another's desire to "figure it out as I go." Because you are such a keen observer of other people's strengths, you can draw out the best in each person. This Individualization theme also helps you build productive teams. While some search around for the perfect team "structure" or "process," you know instinctively that the secret to great teams is casting by individual strengths so that everyone can do a lot of what they do well.

Individualization sounds like this:

Les T., hospitality manager: "Carl is one of our best performers, but he still has to see me every week. He just wants that little encouragement and checking in, and he gets fired up a little bit after that meeting. Whereas Greg doesn't like to meet very often, so there's no need for me to bother him. And when we do meet, it's really for me, not for him."

Marsha D., publishing executive: "Sometimes I would walk out of my office and—you know how cartoon characters have those balloons over their head?—I would see these little balloons over everyone's head telling me what was in their mind. It sounds weird, doesn't it, but it happens all the time."

Giles G., sales manager: "I'm fairly new to this role, but very early on I can remember a particular meeting when we got stuck on one subject and kept going around and around. I got frustrated and suddenly thought, 'These people have never seen me get angry. Let me throw this out and see how each one reacts to it.'

So I got angry, and it was interesting to see how certain people accepted it, some took it as a challenge, and others went into a big shell. Each one's reactions told me something useful about them, something I could use moving forward."

Andrea H., interior designer: "When you ask people what their style is, they find it hard to describe, so I just ask them, 'What is your favorite spot in the house?' And when I ask that, their faces light up, and they know just where to take me. From that one spot I can begin to piece together the kind of people they are and what their style is."

INPUT

You are inquisitive. You collect things. You might collect information—words, facts, books, and quotations—or you might collect tangible objects such as butterflies, baseball cards, porcelain dolls, or sepia photographs. Whatever you collect, you collect it because it interests you. And yours is the kind of mind that finds so many things interesting. The world is exciting precisely because of its infinite variety and complexity. If you read a great deal, it is not necessarily to refine your theories but, rather, to add more information to your archives. If you like to travel, it is because each new location offers novel artifacts and facts. These can be acquired and then stored away. Why are they worth storing? At the time of storing it is often hard to say exactly when or why you might need them, but who knows when they might become useful? With all those possible uses in mind, you really don't feel comfortable throwing anything away. So you keep acquiring and compiling and filing stuff away. It's interesting. It keeps your mind fresh. And perhaps one day some of it will prove valuable.

Input sounds like this:

Ellen K., writer: "Even as a child I found myself wanting to know everything. I would make a game of my questions. 'What is my question today?' I would think up these outrageous questions, and then I would go looking for the books that would answer them. I often got way over my head, deep into books that I didn't have a clue about, but I read them because they had my answer someplace. My questions became my tool for leading me from one piece of information to another."

John F., human resources executive: "I'm one of those people who think that the Internet is the greatest thing since sliced bread. I used to feel so frustrated, but now if I want to know what the stock market is doing in a certain area or the rules of a certain game or what the GNP of Spain is or other different things, I just go to the computer, start looking, and eventually find it."

Kevin F., salesperson: "I'm amazed at some of the garbage that collects in my mind, and I love playing Jeopardy and Trivial Pursuit and anything like that. I don't mind throwing things away as long as they're material things, but I hate wasting knowledge or accumulated knowledge or not being able to read something fully if I enjoy it."

INTELLECTION

You like to think. You like mental activity. You like exercising the "muscles" of your brain, stretching them in multiple directions. This need for mental activity may be focused; for example, you may be trying to solve a problem or develop an idea or understand another person's feelings. The exact focus will depend on your other strengths. On the other hand, this mental activity may very well lack focus. The theme of Intellection does not dictate what you are thinking about; it simply describes that you like to think. You are the kind of person who enjoys your time alone because it is your time for musing and reflection. You are introspective. In a sense you are your own best companion, as you pose yourself questions and try out answers on yourself to see how they sound. This introspection may lead you to a slight sense of discontent as you compare what you are actually doing with all the thoughts and ideas that your mind conceives. Or this introspection may tend toward more pragmatic matters such as the events of the day or a conversation that you plan to have later. Wherever it leads you, this mental hum is one of the constants of your life.

Intellection sounds like this:

Lauren H., project manager: "I suppose that most people who meet me in passing presume that I am a flaming extrovert. I do not deny the fact that I love people, but they would be amazed to know how much time alone, how much solitude I need in order to function in public. I really love my own company. I love solitude because it gives me a chance to allow my diffused focus to simmer with something else. That's where my best ideas come from. My ideas need to simmer and 'perk.' I used this phrase even when I was younger; 'I have put my ideas in, and now I have to wait for them to perk.' "

Michael P., marketing executive: "It's strange, but I find that I need to have noise around me or I can't concentrate. I need to have parts of my brain occupied; otherwise, it goes so fast in so many directions that I don't get anything done. If I can occupy my brain with the TV or my kids running around, then I find I concentrate even better."

Jorge H., factory manager and former political prisoner: "We used to get put into solitary confinement as a punishment, but I never hated it as the others did. You might think that you would get lonely, but I never did. I used the time to reflect on my life and sort out the kind of man I was and what was really important to me, my family, my values. In a weird way solitary actually calmed me down and made me stronger."

LEARNER

You love to learn. The subject matter that interests you most will be determined by your other themes and experiences, but whatever the subject, you will always be drawn to the *process* of learning. The process, more than the content or the result, is especially exciting for you. You are energized by the steady and deliberate journey from ignorance to competence. The thrill of the first few facts, the early efforts to recite or practice what you have learned, the growing confidence of a skill mastered—this is the process that entices you. Your excitement leads you to engage in adult learning experiences—yoga or piano lessons or graduate classes. It enables you to thrive in dynamic work environments where you are asked to take on short project assignments and are expected to learn a lot about the new subject matter in a short period of time and then move on to the next one. This Learner theme does not necessarily mean that you seek to become the subject matter expert, or that you are striving for the respect that accompanies a professional or academic credential. The outcome of the learning is less significant than the "getting there."

Learner sounds like this:

Annie M., managing editor: "I get antsy when I am not learning something. Last year, although I was enjoying my work, I didn't feel as though I was learning enough. So I took up tap dancing. It sounds strange, doesn't it? I know I am never going to perform or anything, but I enjoy focusing on the technical skill of tapping, getting a little better each week, and moving up from the beginners' class to the intermediate class. That was a kick."

Miles A., operations manager: "When I was seven years old, my teachers would tell my parents, 'Miles isn't the most intelligent boy in the school, but he's a sponge for learning and he'll probably go really far because he will push himself and continually be grasping new things.' Right now I am just starting a course in business travel Spanish. I know it is probably too ambitious to think I could learn conversational Spanish and become totally proficient in that language, but I at least want to be able to travel there and know the language."

Tim S., coach for executives: "One of my clients is so

inquisitive that it drives him crazy because he can't do everything he wants to. I'm different. I am not curious in that broad sense. I prefer to go into greater depth with things so that I can become competent in them and then use them at work. For example, recently one of my clients wanted me to travel with him to Nice, France, for a business engagement, so I started reading up on the region, buying books, checking the Internet. It was all interesting and I enjoyed the study, but I wouldn't have done any of it if I wasn't going to be traveling there for work."

MAXIMIZER

Excellence, not average, is your measure. Taking something from below average to slightly above average takes a great deal of effort and in your opinion is not very rewarding. Transforming something strong into something superb takes just as much effort but is much more thrilling. Strengths, whether yours or someone else's, fascinate you. Like a diver after pearls, you search them out, watching for the telltale signs of a strength. A glimpse of untutored excellence, rapid learning, a skill mastered without recourse to steps—all these are clues that a strength may be in play. And having found a strength, you feel compelled to nurture it, refine it, and stretch it toward excellence. You polish the pearl until it shines. This natural sorting of strengths means that others see you as discriminating. You choose to spend time with people who appreciate your particular strengths. Likewise, you are attracted to others who seem to have found and cultivated their own strengths. You tend to avoid those who want to fix you and make you well rounded. You don't want to spend your life bemoaning what you lack. Rather, you want to capitalize on the gifts with which you are blessed. It's more fun. It's more productive. And, counterintuitively, it is more demanding.

Maximizer sounds like this:

Gavin T., flight attendant: "I taught aerobics for ten years, and I made a point of asking people to focus on what they liked about themselves. We all have parts of our body that we would like to change or that we would like to see differently, but to focus on that can be so destructive. It becomes a vicious cycle. So I would say, 'Look, you don't need to be doing that. Instead, let's focus on the attribute you like about yourself, and then we'll all feel better about expending all of this energy.' "

Amy T., magazine editor: "There is nothing I hate more than having to fix a poorly written piece. If I have given the writer a clear focus and she comes back with a piece that is completely off the mark, I almost can't bring myself to write comments on it. I'm more inclined to just hand it back to her and say, 'Just please start again.' On the other hand, what I love to do is take a piece that is so close and then refine it to make it perfect. You know, just the right word here, a little cut there, and suddenly it's a brilliant piece."

Marshall G., marketing executive: "I am really good at setting a focus for people and then building a sense of team spirit as we all march forward. But I am not so good at strategic thinking. Fortunately, I have a boss who understands that about me. We have been working together for quite a few years. He has found people who play the strategic role and at the same time stretched me to be even better at the focus and team-building role. I'm so lucky to have a boss who thinks this way. It's made me more secure and made me charge ahead much faster, knowing that my boss knows what I am good at and what I'm not good at; he doesn't bother me with the latter."

POSITIVITY

You are generous with praise, quick to smile, and always on the lookout for the positive in the situation. Some call you light-hearted. Others just wish that their glass were as full as yours seems to be. But either way, people want to be around you. Their world looks better around you because your enthusiasm is contagious. Lacking your energy and optimism, some find their world drab with repetition or, worse, heavy with pressure. You seem to find a way to lighten their spirit. You inject drama into every project. You celebrate every achievement. You find ways to make everything more exciting and more vital. Some cynics may reject your energy, but you are rarely dragged down. Your Positivity won't allow it. Somehow you can't quite escape your conviction that it is good to be alive, that work can be fun, and that no matter what the setbacks, one must never lose one's sense of humor.

Positivity sounds like this:

Gerry L., flight attendant: "There are so many people on an airplane that I have made it a point over the years of singling out one or two on a flight and making it something special for them. Certainly, I will be courteous to everybody and extend to them the kind of professionalism that I would like given to me, but over and above that I try to make one person or family or small group of people feel particularly special, with jokes and conversation and little games that I play."

Andy B., Internet marketing executive: "I am one of those people who loves creating buzz. I read magazines all the time, and if I find something fun—some new store, new lip gloss, whatever—I will charge around telling everyone about it. 'Oh, you just have to try this store. It is so-o-o cool. Look at these pictures. Check them out.' I am so passionate when I talk about something that people just have to do what I say. It's not that I am a great salesperson. I'm not. In fact, I hate asking for the close, I hate bothering people. It's just that my passion about what I say makes people think, 'Gosh, it must be true.' "

Sunny G., communications manager: "I think the world is plagued with enough negative people. We need more positive people, people who like to zero in on what is right with the world. Negative people just make me feel heavy. In my last job there was a guy who came into my office every morning just to unload on me. I would purposely dodge him. I'd see him coming, and I'd run to the bathroom or go some other place. He made me feel as if the world was a miserable place, and I hated that."

RELATOR

Relator describes your attitude toward your relationships. In simple terms, the Relator theme pulls you toward people you already know. You do not necessarily shy away from meeting new people—in fact, you may have other themes that cause you to enjoy the thrill of turning strangers into friends—but you do derive a great deal of pleasure and strength from being around your close friends. You are comfortable with intimacy. Once the initial connection has been made, you deliberately encourage a deepening of the relationship. You want to understand their feelings, their goals, their fears, and their dreams; and you want them to understand yours. You know that this kind of closeness implies a certain amount of risk—you might be taken advantage of—but you are willing to accept that risk. For you a relationship has value only if it is genuine. And the only way to know that is to entrust yourself to the other person. The more you share with each other, the more you risk together. The more you risk together, the more each of you proves your caring is genuine. These are your steps toward real friendship, and you take them willingly.

Relator sounds like this:

Tony D., pilot: "I used to fly in the Marines, and, boy, you had better be comfortable with the word 'friend' in the Marines. You had better feel good about trusting someone else. I can't tell you how many times I put my life in someone else's hands. I was flying off his wing, and I'd be dead if my friend couldn't get me back safely."

Jamie T., entrepreneur: "I'm definitely selective about my relationships. Initially, when I first meet people, I don't want to give them very much of my time. I don't know them, they don't know me, so let's just be pleasant and leave it at that. But if circumstances make it so that we get to know each other better, it seems like a threshold is reached where I suddenly start wanting to invest more. I'll share more of myself, put myself out for them, do things for them that will bring us a little closer together and show that I care. It's funny because I am not looking for any more friends in my life. I have enough. And yet with each new person I meet, as soon as that threshold is reached, I feel compelled to go deeper and deeper. Now I have ten people working for me, and I would call each of them my very good friend."

Gavin T., flight attendant: "I have many wonderful acquaintances, but as for true friends that I hold dear, not very many. And I'm real okay with that. My best times are spent with the people I'm tightest with, like my family. We are a very tight-knit Irish Catholic family, and we get together every chance we can. It's a large family—I have five brothers and sisters and ten nieces and nephews—but we all get together about once a month and yuk it up. I'm the catalyst. When I'm back in Chicago, even if there is no birthday or anniversary or whatever, I become the excuse for getting together and hanging out for three or four days. We really enjoy one another's company."

RESPONSIBILITY

Your Responsibility theme forces you to take psychological ownership for anything you commit to, and whether large or small, you feel emotionally bound to follow it through to completion. Your good name depends on it. If for some reason you cannot deliver, you automatically start to look for ways to make it up to the other person. Apologies are not enough. Excuses and rationalizations are totally unacceptable. You will not quite be able to live with yourself until you have made restitution. This conscientiousness, this near obsession for doing things right, and your impeccable ethics, combine to create your reputation: utterly dependable. When assigning new responsibilities, people will look to you first because they know it will get done. When people come to you for help—and they soon will—you must be selective. Your willingness to volunteer may sometimes lead you to take on more than you should.

Responsibility sounds like this:

Harry B., outplacement consultant: "I was just a young bank manager in one of the branches when the president of the company decided that he wanted to foreclose on a property. I said, 'That's fine, but we have a responsibility to give the people full value for their property.' He didn't see it that way. He wanted to sell the property to a friend of his for what was owed, and he said my problem was that I couldn't separate my business ethics from my personal ethics. I told him that was correct. I couldn't because I didn't believe and still don't believe that you can have two standards. So I quit the firm and went back to earning $5 an hour working for the forestry service picking up trash. Since my wife and I were trying to support our two kids and make ends meet, it was a hard decision for me to make. But looking back, on one level it really wasn't hard at all. I simply couldn't function in an organization with those kinds of ethics."

Kelly G., operations manager: "The country manager in Sweden called me in November and said, 'Kelly, could you please not ship my inventory until January 1.' I said, 'Sure. Sounds like a good plan.' I told my people of the plan and thought I had all the bases covered. On December 31, however, when I was checking my messages while on a ski slope, making sure everything was hunky-dory, I saw that his order had already been shipped and invoiced. I had to call immediately and tell him what happened. He's a nice man, so he didn't use any four-letter words, but he was very angry and very disappointed. I felt terrible. An apology wasn't enough. I needed to fix it. I called our controller from the chalet, and that afternoon we figured out a way to put the value of his inventory back on our books and clean it off his. It took most of the weekend, but it was the right thing to do."

Nigel T., sales executive: "I used to think that there was a piece of metal in my hand and a magnet on the ceiling. I would just volunteer for everything. I have had to learn how to manage that because not only would I end up with too much on my plate, but I would also wind up thinking that everything was my fault. I realize now that I can't be responsible for everything in the world—that's God's job."

RESTORATIVE

You love to solve problems. Whereas some are dismayed when they encounter yet another breakdown, you can be energized by it. You enjoy the challenge of analyzing the symptoms, identifying what is wrong, and finding the solution. You may prefer practical problems or conceptual ones or personal ones. You may seek out specific kinds of problems that you have met many times before and that you are confident you can fix. Or you may feel the greatest push when faced with complex and unfamiliar problems. Your exact preferences are determined by your other themes and experiences. But what is certain is that you enjoy bringing things back to life. It is a wonderful feeling to identify the undermining factor(s), eradicate them, and restore something to its true glory. Intuitively, you know that without your intervention, this thing—this machine, this technique, this person, this company—might have ceased to function. You fixed it, resuscitated it, rekindled its vitality. Phrasing it the way you might, you saved it.

Restorative sounds like this:

Nigel L., software designer: "I have these vivid memories of my childhood woodworking bench with hammers and nails and wood. I used to love fixing things and putting things together and making everything just so. And now with computer programs it's the same thing. You write the program, and if it doesn't work, you have to go back and redo it and fix it until it works."

Jan K., internist: "This theme plays in my life in so many ways. For example, my first love was surgery. I love trauma, love being in the OR, love sewing. I just love fixing things in the OR. Then again, some of my best moments have been sitting at the bedside of a dying patient, just talking together. It is incredibly rewarding to watch someone make the transition from anger to acceptance about grief, to tie up loose ends with family members, and to pass with dignity. And then with my kids this theme fires every day. When I see my three-year-old buttoning her sweater for the first time and she buttons it crooked, I feel this powerful urge to walk up and rebutton the sweater. I have to resist, of course, because she has to learn, but, boy, it's really hard."

Marie T., television producer: "Producing a morning TV program is a fundamentally clumsy process. If I didn't like solving problems, this job would drive me up the wall. Every day something serious goes wrong, and I have to find the problem, fix it, and move on to the next one. If I can do that well, I feel rejuvenated. On the other hand, if I go home and a problem remains unsolved, then I feel the opposite. I feel defeated."

SELF-ASSURANCE

Self-assurance is similar to self-confidence. In the deepest part of you, you have faith in your strengths. You *know* that you are able—able to take risks, able to meet new challenges, able to stake claims, and, most important, able to deliver. But Self-assurance is more than just self-confidence. Blessed with the theme of Self-assurance, you have confidence not only in your abilities but in your judgment. When you look at the world, you know that your perspective is unique and distinct. And because no one sees exactly what you see, you know that no one can make your decisions for you. No one can tell you what to think. They can guide. They can suggest. But you alone have the authority to form conclusions, make decisions, and act. This authority, this final accountability for the living of your life, does not intimidate you. On the contrary, it feels natural to you. No matter what the situation, you seem to know what the right decision is. This theme lends you an aura of certainty. Unlike many, you are not easily swayed by someone else's arguments, no matter how persuasive they may be. This Self-assurance may be quiet or loud, depending on your other themes, but it is solid. It is strong. Like the keel of a ship, it withstands many different pressures and keeps you on your course.

Self-assurance sounds like this:

Pam D., public service executive: "I was raised on a remote farm in Idaho, and I attended a small rural school. One day I returned home from school and announced to my mother that I was changing schools. Earlier in the day my teacher had explained that our school had too many kids and that three kids would have to move to a different school. I thought about it for a moment, liked the idea of meeting new people, and decided I would be one of them—even though it meant getting up half an hour earlier and traveling further on the bus. I was five years old."

James K., salesman: "I never second-guess myself. Whether I am buying a birthday present or a house, when I make my decision, it feels to me as if I had no choice. There was only one decision to make, and I made it. It's easy for me to sleep at night. My gut is final, loud, and very persuasive."

Deborah C., ER nurse: "If we have a death in the ER, people call on me to deal with the family because of my confidence. Just yesterday we had a problem with a young psychotic girl who was screaming that the devil was inside her. The other nurses were afraid, but I knew what to do. I went in and said, 'Kate, come on, lie back. Let's say the Baruch. It's a Jewish prayer. It goes like this: Baruch Atah Adonai, Eloheinu Melech Haolam.' She responded, 'Say it slowly so that I can say it back to you.' I did and then she said it back to me slowly. She wasn't Jewish, but this calm came over her. She dropped back against her pillow and said, 'Thank you. That's all I needed.' "

SIGNIFICANCE

You want to be very significant in the eyes of other people. In the truest sense of the word you want to be recognized. You want to be heard. You want to stand out. You want to be known. In particular, you want to be known and appreciated for the unique strengths you bring. You feel a need to be admired as credible, professional, and successful. Likewise, you want to associate with others who are credible, professional, and successful. And if they aren't, you will push them to achieve until they are. Or you will move on. An independent spirit, you want your work to be a way of life rather than a job, and in that work you want to be given free rein, the leeway to do things your way. Your yearnings feel intense to you, and you honor those yearnings. And so your life is filled with goals, achievements, or qualifications that you crave. Whatever your focus—and each person is distinct—your Significance theme will keep pulling you upward, away from the mediocre toward the exceptional. It is the theme that keeps you reaching.

Significance sounds like this:

Mary P., healthcare executive: "Women are told almost from day one, 'Don't be too proud. Don't stand tall.' That kind of thing. But I've learned that it's okay to have power, it's okay to have pride, and it's okay to have a big ego. And also that I need to manage it and drive it in the right directions."

Kathie J., partner in a law firm: "Ever since I can remember I have had the feeling that I was special, that I could take charge and make things happen. Back in the sixties I was the first woman partner in my firm, and I can still recall walking into boardroom after boardroom and being the only woman. It's strange, thinking back. It was tough, but I actually think I enjoyed the pressure of standing out. I enjoyed being the 'woman' partner. Why? Because I knew that I would be very hard to forget. I knew everyone would notice me and pay attention to me."

John L., physician: "All through my life I felt that I was onstage. I am *always* aware of an audience. If I am sitting with a patient, I want the patient to see me as the best doctor he or she has ever had. If I am teaching medical students, I want to stand out as the best medical educator they have ever had. I want to win the Educator of the Year Award. My boss is a big audience for me. Disappointing her would kill me. It's scary to think that part of my self-esteem is in other people's hands, but then again, it keeps me on my toes."

STRATEGIC

The Strategic theme enables you to sort through the clutter and find the best route. It is not a skill that can be taught. It is a distinct way of thinking, a special perspective on the world at large. This perspective allows you to see patterns where others simply see complexity. Mindful of these patterns, you play out alternative scenarios, always asking, "What if this happened? Okay, well what if this happened?" This recurring question helps you see around the next corner. There you can evaluate accurately the potential obstacles. Guided by where you see each path leading, you start to make selections. You discard the paths that lead nowhere. You discard the paths that lead straight into resistance. You discard the paths that lead into a fog of confusion. You cull and make selections until you arrive at the chosen path—your strategy. Armed with your strategy, you strike forward. This is your Strategic theme at work: "What if?" Select. Strike.

Strategic sounds like this:

Liam C., manufacturing plant manager: "It seems as if I

can always see the consequences before anyone else can. I have to say to people, 'Lift up your eyes, look down the road a ways. Let's talk about where we are going to be next year so that when we get to this time next year, we don't have the same problems.' It seems obvious to me, but some people are just too focused on this month's numbers, and everything is driven by that."

Vivian T., television producer: "I used to love logic problems when I was a kid. You know, the ones where 'if A implies B, and B equals C, does A equal C?' Still today I am always playing out repercussions, seeing where things lead. I think it makes me a great interviewer. I know that nothing is an accident; every sign, every word, every tone of voice has significance. So I watch for these clues and play them out in my head, see where they lead, and then plan my questions to take advantage of what I have seen in my head."

Simon T., human resources executive: "We really needed to take the union on at some stage, and I saw an opportunity, a very good issue to take them on. I could see that they were going in a direction that would lead them into all kinds of trouble if they continued down it. Lo and behold, they did continue down it, and when they arrived, there I was, ready and waiting. I suppose it just comes naturally to me to predict what someone else is going to do. And then when that person reacts, I can respond immediately because I have sat down and said, 'Okay, if they do this, we'll do this. If they do that, then we'll do this other thing.' It's like when you tack in a sailboat. You head in one direction, but you jink one way, then another, planning and reacting, planning and reacting."

WOO

Woo stands for winning others over. You enjoy the challenge of meeting new people and getting them to like you. Strangers are rarely intimidating to you. On the contrary, strangers can be energizing. You are drawn to them. You want to learn their names, ask them questions, and find some area of common interest so that you can strike up a conversation and build rapport. Some people shy away from starting up conversations because they worry about running out of things to say. You don't. Not only are you rarely at a loss for words, but you actually enjoy initiating with strangers because you derive satisfaction from breaking the ice and making a connection. Once that connection is made, you are quite happy to wrap it up and move on. There are new people to meet, new rooms to work, new crowds to mingle in. In your world there are no strangers, only friends you haven't met yet— lots of them.

Woo sounds like this:

Deborah C., publishing executive: "I have made best friends out of people that I have met passing in the doorway. I mean it's awful, but wooing is part of who I am. All my taxi drivers propose to me."

Marilyn K., college president: "I don't believe I'm looking for friends, but people call me a friend. I call people and say, 'I love you,' and I mean it because I love people easily. But friends? I don't have many friends. I don't think I am looking for friends. I am looking for connections. And I am really good at that because I know how to achieve common ground with people."

Anna G., nurse: "I think I am a little shy sometimes. Usually I won't make the first step out. But I do know how to put people at ease. A lot of my job is just humor. If the patient is not very receptive, my role becomes a stand-up comedian. I'll say to an eighty-year-old patient, 'Hi, you handsome guy. Sit up. Let me get your shirt off. That's good. Take your shirt off. Whoa, what a chest on this man!' With kids you have to start very slowly and say something like 'How old are you?' If they say 'ten,' then you say, 'Really? When I was your age, I was eleven'—silly stuff like that to break the ice."

III

Put Strengths to Work

CHAPTER **5**

The Questions You're Asking

- ARE THERE ANY OBSTACLES TO BUILDING MY STRENGTHS?
- WHY SHOULD I FOCUS ON MY SIGNATURE THEMES?
- IS THERE ANY SIGNIFICANCE TO THE ORDER OF MY SIGNATURE THEMES?
- NOT ALL OF THE PHRASES IN THE THEME DESCRIPTION APPLY TO ME. WHY?
- WHY AM I DIFFERENT FROM OTHER PEOPLE WITH WHOM I SHARE SOME OF THE SAME THEMES?
- ARE ANY OF THE THEMES "OPPOSITES"?
- CAN I DEVELOP NEW THEMES IF I DON'T LIKE THE ONES I HAVE?
- WILL I BECOME TOO NARROW IF I FOCUS ON MY SIGNATURE THEMES?
- HOW CAN I MANAGE AROUND MY WEAKNESSES?
- CAN MY THEMES REVEAL WHETHER I AM IN THE RIGHT CAREER?

YOU have taken the StrengthsFinder Profile. You have received your top five themes and read the descriptions and the quotes. And now, if you react as most people do, you will have quite a few questions running through your head. From past experience we have determined the questions most frequently asked, and we trust that our answers will address your most pressing queries.

Are There Any Obstacles to Building My Strengths?

Yes. Aside from the policies of your organization (which we shall address in the last chapter), there is one obstacle barring your progress: Your own reluctance.

This probably sounds strange. Why would anyone be reluctant to build on their strengths? The truth is that many people are reluctant. Many people don't concern themselves with the intricacies of their strengths; instead, they choose to devote their time and energy to investigating their weaknesses. We know this because we asked them this question: "Which do you think will help you improve the most: knowing your strengths or knowing your weaknesses?"

Whether we asked the question of the American population, the British, the French, the Canadian, the Japanese, or the Chinese, whether the people were young or old, rich or poor, highly educated or less so, the answer was always the same: weaknesses, not strengths, deserve the most attention. Admittedly, we did discover quite a wide range of responses to this question. The most strengths-focused culture is the United States, with 41 percent of the population saying that knowing their strengths will help them improve the most. The least strengths-focused cultures are Japan and China. Only 24 percent believe that the key to success lies in their strengths. However, despite the range, this general conclusion holds true: The majority of the world's population doesn't think that the secret to improvement lies in a deep understanding of their strengths. (Interestingly, in every culture the group least fixated on their weaknesses was the oldest group, those fifty-five years old and above. A little older, a little wiser, this group has probably acquired a measure of self-acceptance and realized the futility of trying to paper over the persistent cracks in their personality.)

Of all the research we conducted for this book, these discoveries were perhaps the most surprising. They require an explanation. Why do so many people avoid focusing on their strengths? Why do weaknesses prove so mesmerizing? Unless we face up to these questions and resolve them now, your efforts to build your strengths might peter out before they have had a chance to gain momentum.

There are as many reasons as there are people to concoct them, but all these reasons seem to stem from the same three basic fears: fear of weaknesses, fear of failure, and, fear of one's true self.

FEAR OF WEAKNESSES

For many of us our fear of our weaknesses seems to overshadow our confidence in our strengths. To use an analogy, if life is a game of cards and each of us has been dealt our hand of strengths and weaknesses, most of us assume that our weaknesses trump our strengths.

For example, if we excel at selling but struggle with strategy, it is our difficulty with strategy that gets the attention because an inability to think strategically will surely hurt us somewhere down the line, won't it? If we build trusting relationships with ease but falter when it comes to making presentations, we sign up for the ubiquitous public speaking class because public speaking is a prerequisite for success, isn't it? Whatever the weakness, whatever the strength, the strength is just a strength—to be admired and then simply assumed—but the weakness, ah, the weakness is an "area of opportunity."

This fixation with weakness is deeply rooted in our education and upbringing. We presented parents with this scenario: Say your child returns home with the following grades: an A in English, an A in social studies, a C in biology, and an F in algebra. Which of these grades would you spend the most time discussing with your son or daughter? Seventy-seven percent of parents chose to focus on the F in algebra, only 6 percent on the A in English, and an even more minuscule number, 1 percent, on the A in social studies. Obviously, the algebra grade requires some attention because to progress in school and secure a place at a college or university, the child cannot afford to fail a subject. But the question was phrased quite carefully: Which of these grades would you spend the *most* time discussing with your son or daughter? Despite the demands of today's education system, does the most time really deserve to be invested in the child's weakness?

This weakness orientation persists in the fields of research and academia. In a recent speech to his professional colleagues, Martin Seligman, past president of the American Psychological Association, reported that he had found over forty thousand studies on depression but only forty on the subject of joy, happiness, or fulfillment. As with the algebra example, the point here is not that depression should not be studied. Depression is a deadening disease, and those who suffer from it need all the help that science can offer them. (In fact, as a result of science's passionate focus on mental illness during the last half century, treatments for fourteen distinct mental illnesses have been discovered.) The point is that our balance is off. Our perspective is so skewed toward weakness and illness that we know precious little about strength and health. In Martin Seligman's words, "Psychology is half-baked, literally half-baked. We have baked the part about mental illness. We have baked the part about repair and damage. But the other side is unbaked. The side of strengths, the side of what we are good at, the side . . . of what makes life worth living."

Each of us has weaknesses, of course. Activities that are effortless for some may be frustratingly difficult for us. And if these weaknesses interfere with our strengths, we need to develop strategies to manage around them (we will list these strategies in full later in the chapter). To clear our skewed perspective, however, we must remember that casting a critical eye on our weaknesses and working hard to manage them, while sometimes necessary, will only help us prevent failure. It will not help us reach excellence. What Seligman is saying—and what many of the excellent performers we interviewed are telling us—is that you will reach excellence only by understanding and cultivating your strengths.

Back in the 1930s, Carl Jung, the eminent thinker and psychologist, put it this way: Criticism has "the power to do good when there is something that must be destroyed, dissolved or reduced, but [it is] capable only of harm when there is something to be built."

FEAR OF FAILURE

This is the usual suspect in the sense that because failing is never fun, some of us choose not to risk it. But in the context of the challenges of strong living, this fear of failure becomes particularly resilient and difficult to dislodge.

All failures are not created equal. Some are fairly easy to digest, usually those where we can explain away the failure without tarnishing our self-image. It may sound a little different in kindergarten ("Hey, I wasn't ready!") than it does in the working world ("I'm afraid that's not my specialty"), but the principle is the same. When the cause of the failure seems to have nothing to do with who we really are, we can accept it.

But some failures stick in our throat and lodge there. Of this kind the most persistent and the most damaging are those times when we pick out one of our strengths, stake a claim, go all out, and yet still fail. The anguish that accompanies this kind of failure can be acute. Do you remember the scene in the film *Chariots of Fire* where the runner Abrahams turns to his girlfriend after losing a race for which he had prepared diligently and in a stunned whisper confesses, "I just don't think I can run any faster"?

Whether we are competitive like Abrahams or judge ourselves against our own standards, our sense of failure is most pervasive whenever we reach down, call upon our strengths, and they are found wanting. Despite society's well-intentioned advice to "try, try again," at times like these we can start to feel a little desperate. "I identified a talent, cultivated it into a strength, claimed it, practiced it, and still failed! So where do I turn now?"

An added twist to this fear of a strength-based failure is that society reserves its most delighted ridicule for those who claim strengths and then fail. Think of Donald Trump's highly public brush with bankruptcy in the early 1990s. Think of Richard Branson's struggles to launch Virgin Cola. There are probably very few of us who, hand on heart, can say that we did not take just a smidgen of pleasure in seeing such grand claims fall short. Our baser instincts encourage us to take pleasure in another's misfortunes; unfortunately, the pleasure seems to increase in direct proportion to the other person's ego. The bigger his ego, the greater our pleasure in his failure.

For both of these reasons, then, many of us avoid the exposure of building on our strengths. Instead, we stay in the workroom patching up the cracks. It is diligent, it is humble, and society respects it. Unfortunately, as we just described, patching up your weaknesses will never lead you to excellence. So what should you do? How can you overcome this potent fear of strength-based failure?

Well, more than likely you will never entirely dissolve either your fear of your own failure or your small pleasure in other people's. Both seem to be ingrained in those aspects of human nature many of us share. By examining them up close, however, you can at least demystify them to such an extent that neither stops you from building on your strengths.

Let's start with the ego problem. Is it egotistical to spend your life building on your strengths? Everything we know from our research says that it isn't. Building on your strengths and egotism are not the same thing. Egotism is when you make claims to excellence, but your claims aren't tied to anything substantive. This blustering, "big hat, no cattle" approach to life is ripe for ridicule.

But building on your strengths isn't necessarily about ego. It is about responsibility. You should not take pride in your natural talents any more than you should take pride in your sex, race, or the color of your hair. Your natural talents are gifts from God or accidents of birth, depending on the articles of your faith. Either way, you had nothing to do with them. However, you have a great deal to do with fashioning them into strengths. It is your opportunity to take your natural talents and transform them through focus and practice and learning into consistent near perfect performances.

From this point of view, to avoid your strengths and to focus on your weaknesses isn't a sign of diligent humility. It is almost irresponsible. By contrast the most responsible, the most challenging, and, in the sense of being true to yourself, the most honorable thing to do is face up to the strength potential inherent in your talents and then find ways to realize it.

Might you fail? Yes, you might. Building a strong life means that you allow performance to be the final judge of your strengths. Performance, properly measured, is implacable and unforgiving, and without doubt there will be times when your claims of strength are judged unfavorably.

So what? Really, what is the worst that could happen? So you identify a talent, cultivate it into a strength, and fail to perform up to your expectations. Yes, it hurts, but it shouldn't undermine you completely. It is a chance to learn and to incorporate this learning into your next performance, and your next. And what if these next performances still fail to meet your standards? Well, it hurts some more. But it should also tell you something: You might be searching for your strengths in the wrong places. Despite the hurt, you are at least freed up to redirect your search more productively. As the wit W. C. Fields advised: "If at first you don't succeed, try again. Then quit. There is no point making a fool of yourself."

This advice is easy to give and difficult to put into practice, but as you build your strengths, sometimes making great progress, sometimes slipping back, take comfort from the fact that this is how a strong life is supposed to be lived. This process—act, learn, refine, act, learn, refine—clumsy though it may be, is the essence of strong living. Strong living asks you to be bold, to be perceptive, to listen for performance feedback from the outside world, and, above all, to keep investigating your strengths despite the many influences pulling you away from them. Again, Carl Jung captured the spirit of it best when he said: "Fidelity to the law of your own being is . . . an act of high courage flung in the face of life."

A word of warning: Be on the lookout for the one menacing danger that can undermine you: delusion. This occurs when you keep acting, keep failing, and don't realize it. You think that you have a strength in public speaking, yet you don't realize the audience is zoning out. Or you imagine yourself a superstar salesperson, yet never wonder why nobody buys. Or you see yourself as the greatest manager of people since Vince Lombardi, yet never notice that your employees steer clear of you as you patrol the hallways. Or, most dangerous of all, you dimly register your poor performances, yet somehow seem to find a million reasons why it has nothing to do with you. Delusion plus denial is a lethal combination.

If you are thus afflicted, nothing in this book will cure you. All we can tell you is that the person you are doing the most harm to is yourself. The philosopher Baruch Spinoza said that "to be what we are, and to become what we are capable of becoming, is the only end of life." You may disagree with his emphasis, but surely one of the goals of your life is to discover and apply your strengths. If your senses are numbed with delusion and denial, you will stop looking for these true strengths and wind up living a second-rate version of someone else's life rather than a world-class version of your own.

FEAR OF ONE'S TRUE SELF

You may be reluctant to investigate your strengths quite simply because you don't believe that your true self is much to write home about. Whatever the label—a feeling of inadequacy or "imposter syndrome" or plain old insecurity—the symptoms are familiar. Despite your achievements, you wonder whether you are as talented as everyone thinks you are. You suspect that luck and circumstance, not your strengths, might explain much of your success. The anxious little voice in your ear whispers, "When will you be found out?" and, against your better judgment, you listen.

In part this explains why, when asked to describe their strengths, people rarely refer to their natural talents. Instead, they talk about external things that they have gathered during their life, such as certificates and diplomas, experiences and awards. Here is the "proof" that they have improved themselves, that they have acquired something valuable to offer.

We don't mean to imply that this fear is entirely negative. After all, the flip side of insecurity is complacency. We do want to remind you, however, that if you stop investigating yourself for fear of how little you might find, you will miss the wonder of your strengths. We say "remind" because so many of us take our strengths for granted. We live with them every day, and they come so easily to us that they cease to be precious. Like the New Yorker who no longer hears the sirens and the horns, we are so close to our strengths that we don't see them anymore.

A few years ago Bruce B. won one of America's most prestigious award for teachers. According to feedback from his peers, his students, and their parents, he was brilliant at creating a focused yet caring environment for learning. As part of Gallup's study of excellence, we interviewed him and then gave him feedback on his strengths. One of his strongest talents was Empathy, so we talked to him about how powerful it was that he could pick up on the feelings of each student, that he could make each one feel heard and understood. We described how this theme enabled him to hear the unspoken questions, to anticipate each student's learning hurdles, and to tailor his teaching style so that together they could find a way around them. We painted as vivid a picture as we could of how he had cultivated this talent into a tremendous strength.

When we were done, Bruce sat there with a strange look on his face. He wasn't surprised. He wasn't intrigued. He didn't even seem particularly flattered. He was just confused.

"Doesn't everyone do that?" he asked.

The answer, of course, was "No. Everyone doesn't do that, but you do, Bruce. You do. It's what makes you so very good at what you do. If every teacher was as empathic as you, every teacher would be as good as you. And they aren't."

Bruce had fallen into the trap that catches so many of us. He couldn't help but spot the clues that revealed each student's emotional state. He couldn't help but respond to the emotions he saw. He couldn't help but share their pain and rejoice in their successes. And because he couldn't help it, he didn't value it. It was easy, and so it was mundane, commonplace, obvious. "Doesn't everybody do that?"

The old maxim says that you can't see the picture when you are inside the frame. Well, you spend your whole life inside the frame of your strengths, so perhaps it is little wonder that after a while you become blind to them. We hope that by revealing your five signature themes we have shown you that your instinctive reactions to the world around you—those things that "you can't help but . . ."—are not mundane, commonplace, obvious. On the contrary, your instinctive reactions are unique. They make you different from everyone else. They make you extraordinary.

Why Should I Focus on My Signature Themes?

The chief purpose of StrengthsFinder is not to sum you up or to offer a full character portrait. Instead, the point of the Strengths-Finder Profile is to help you achieve consistent near perfect performance—performance that is both excellent and fulfilling. This kind of strength building requires a sharp focus for a couple of reasons.

First, although you have undoubtedly experienced some moments of success and fulfillment in your life, the secret to strong living lies in being able to replicate these moments time and again. To do this you need to understand these moments deeply. You need to discern which strengths were in play and how they combined to create either the performance or the satisfaction or both. You need to be *consciously competent*. To achieve this conscious competence with even five themes of talent is quite a challenge.

Second, when you look closely, the difference between someone whose performance is acceptable and someone whose performance is consistently near perfect is very slight. The near perfect performer is rarely doing something dramatically different. Confronted by the daily barrage of a thousand instantaneous decisions, he is simply making a very small number of more appropriate choices.

How small a number? Well, in baseball if you hit the ball successfully 270 times for every thousand plate appearances, you will be a middling player. If you can manage 320 hits per thousand, you will be hailed as one of the league's best. So in baseball the difference between middle of the road and superstardom is about twenty-five better decisions per season (on average, a batter will make 500 plate appearances a season). In professional golf the difference between excellence and average is similarly slight. The top players average twenty-seven putts per round. The middling players average thirty-two.

In the world of work, the difference between the struggling salesperson and the great one might be just three extra calls made each week or two more emotional signals picked up during a presentation or one more fact tossed in at just the right moment of a conversation. The difference between the exemplary mentor and the run-of-the-mill boss might simply be a few more questions asked and a few more moments spent listening. No matter what your profession, the secret to consistent near perfect performance lies in these kinds of subtle refinements.

To achieve these refinements demands expertise. You will need to study your strongest themes of talent and figure out how they combine to create your strengths. Pondering them in this way, you may suddenly realize that a small shift in emphasis from one theme to another or a deepening of your knowledge in one particular area is all you need to help you make the leap from middling to excellent performance.

For example, if one of your signature themes is Input, you may realize that although you read a great deal, you don't discipline yourself to archive interesting articles and facts. So you decide to make a slight change in your weekly regimen. You create a clipping file and reread everything in it at least once a quarter. You quickly discover that with this wealth of information fresh in your mind, you are more insightful, more helpful, and more creative.

Or perhaps, with Connectedness as one of your signature themes, you have always felt the comfort that this theme brings you in your personal life, but you have never thought to apply it in your professional life. So now you make an adjustment. You deliberately talk to your colleagues about how each of their efforts is combined to create the team's total performance. You highlight how one person's attention to detail makes another's work that much easier. You emphasize the common purpose and the need for mutual support.

As a result, you gradually build your reputation as one of the best team builders in the company.

To polish even one theme so that it becomes a true strength will test your self-awareness and your resourcefulness. To hone all five is the work of a lifetime.

Is There Any Significance to the Order of My Signature Themes?

Technically, the answer is yes, but in practical terms, no. The StrengthsFinder Profile evaluates each of your responses, calculates your strongest themes, and presents your top five in descending order. Thus, technically, the first theme listed is your strongest theme. The fifth theme listed is your fifth strongest.

However, we advise you not to place too much emphasis on the order of your signature themes. First, the actual difference between your number one theme and your number five theme, and those in between, may well be infinitesimally small. In the world of mathematics, the differences exist, but in the real world, they may be meaningless.

Second, the practical purpose of StrengthsFinder is to highlight your *dominant* patterns of thought, feeling, or behavior. Here we are drawing a distinction between your signature themes and your responsive themes. Your signature themes are those that you lead with. No matter what the situation, they filter your world, forcing you to behave in certain recurring ways. By contrast, your responsive themes fire only occasionally, usually when a very particular situation presents itself.

For example, if one of your signature themes is Developer, you will actively look for opportunities to set other people up for success. Their growth will always be on your mind. If Developer is a responsive theme, it will kick in only when the other person is sitting in front of you asking for your advice on her career. Similarly, if Strategic thinking is a signature theme you will approach every situation by asking "What if?" Whether standing in the shower or jogging or lying awake late at night, your mind will not be able to stop itself from its instinctive contingency planning. However, if Strategic is a responsive theme, it will be switched on only when the time comes to carve the five-year business plan.

Responsive themes can come in handy sometimes because they enable you to perform acceptably well as long as everything is cued up for you, but your signature themes don't rely on cues. They are powerful precisely because they are instinctual. Each of them, one through five, is a self-starting theme and is a critical component in strength building.

Not All of the Phrases in the Theme Description Apply to Me. Why?

In a sense the thirty-four themes do not actually exist. Achiever cannot be found in one corner of a person's brain and Belief in another. Each person's recurring patterns of thought, feeling, or behavior are created by the threads in his network. Some are strong. Some are broken. For all the obvious reasons—genetic inheritance, upbringing, culture—a person's network is unique.

When Gallup interviewed the two million excellent performers to learn about human strengths, we were investigating the unique configuration of each individual's network. By contrast, when we decided to summarize our research and create a common language for explaining human strengths, we had to ignore this uniqueness. Instead, we wove the most common threads into patterns, and these patterns then became the thirty-four themes of StrengthsFinder. In the descriptions we have tried to capture the most prevalent threads of each pattern or theme, but because each theme is a summary, it is likely that some of the threads will not resonate with you as strongly as others do.

To stretch the analogy, the themes are patterns in the same way that tartan, paisley, and herringbone are patterns. Every herringbone jacket contains slightly different threads, but each is recognizable as herringbone. Likewise, if you possess the theme Competition, you may be drawn to contests that are different from others who have this same theme, but in the contests that matter to each of you, you will not label yourselves "good losers."

Why Am I Different from Other People with Whom I Share Some of the Same Themes?

Very few people share your signature themes (in fact, there are over thirty-three million possible combinations of the top five, so the chances of your meeting your perfect match are infinitesimal). This is relevant because none of your five themes stands alone. Rather, each theme is so interwoven with every other one that it is modified, altered by association. The following progression of theme pairs serves as an example of how, by substituting only one theme in the pair, the overall pattern of behavior changes dramatically.

The theme Ideation describes a love of ideas and connections. The theme Context describes an instinctive need to investigate how things came to be the way they are. Together they produce a creative theorist who takes the time to look to the past for clues to explain the present. In the extreme, picture Charles Darwin wondering why the beaks of Galapagos finches varied in shape and size, and starting to see the outline of his theory of natural selection.

Now make one change. Keep Ideation but substitute Futuristic—a fascination with the potential of the future—for Context. Ideation and Futuristic together create a visionary dreamer who can distill from the present key trends and then project how these trends will come together ten years hence. Think of Bill Gates, chairman of Microsoft, and his vivid goal of a computer in every household.

Now keep Futuristic but for Ideation substitute Belief, a need to orient one's life around a core set of values, usually altruistic. The Futuristic and Belief themes also create a visionary dreamer, but his dreams tend to be very different from the previous example.

Whereas Bill Gates and his ilk imagine a better world, the Futuristic/Belief dreamer can't help but imagine a better world *for people*. He is less concerned about the creativity of his dream and more concerned about its beneficial impact. Dr. Martin Luther King, Jr., is probably the most compelling example. He not only oriented his life around the value of racial equality but projected this value into a vivid picture of the future, a future where a black girl and a white boy could drink from the same water fountain, sit in the same classrooms, and walk hand in hand down the same street.

Lastly, keep Belief but for Futuristic substitute Relator, a desire to get to know people well and to build close relationships with them. The Belief and Relator themes combine to create a missionary, not a visionary. This person has little time for inspirational images, which are too distant, too ethereal. Instead, she wants to meet the people she is helping. She wants to learn their names and understand their unique situations. Only then can she be sure that she is indeed living out her values. This person recalls the spirit of Mother Teresa rather than that of Martin Luther King, Jr.

Since we have jumped from Charles Darwin to Mother Teresa by simply switching one theme, you can see why your behavior may be significantly different from people who share one, two, three, or even four of your signature themes. So try not to examine each of your themes in isolation. Instead, examine how each modifies the others. Figure out the combination effects. Therein lies the secret to real self-awareness.

Are Any of the Themes "Opposites"?

The answer to this question is no. Personality tests tend to be based on the assumption that many human traits are mutually exclusive. For example, you can be either an introvert or an extrovert, but never both. You can be either ego-driven or altruistic; either assertive or agreeable; either future-oriented or nostalgic. This either/or assumption is then built into these questionnaires. Each question is designed so that a positive score for one trait automatically ensures a negative score on the opposite trait. Such questions are labeled "ipsative," which means that if in reality you have both, the question makes it impossible for you to show up with both.

The StrengthsFinder Profile is not built this way for the simple reason that this either/or assumption doesn't seem to play out in the real world. During our interviews we found hundreds of thousands of people who possessed themes that at first glance would be considered opposites. David G., the president of a film company in Hollywood, displayed the dominant themes of both Woo (a love of the challenge of winning others over) and Intellection (a need for time alone to ponder and ruminate). His Woo theme enabled him to make hundreds of calls a day in his quest to charm desirable film projects onto his lot. His Intellection theme lent him a reflective air and, not insignificantly, allowed him to relate to the interior life of the characters he read and of the writers who wrote them. When we asked David about this seeming inconsistency, he said that the combination of Woo and Intellection made perfect sense to him. "I am the kind of guy who dreads going to parties but who is suddenly at my best once I'm there."

With the following example, Leslie T., an investment banker, revealed two of her strongest but seemingly "opposite" themes, Harmony (a willingness to avoid conflict if at all possible) and

Command (a need to confront). "As president of my home owners association I had to supervise the bidding process for a neighborhood landscaping project. Because it was quite a large contract, I wanted to run the bidding process myself. However, one of my board members stood up at the meeting and argued that he should run it because he knew the business, had friends in construction, the whole bit. I would have stuck to my guns, but he was so adamant that I let it slide and gave him the okay. But then a month later, after I saw the final contract, I discovered that he hadn't even opened the contract up for bid. He had simply waited until the last minute and then handed the contract to a friend of his. I was furious. Situations like this can be difficult because it's not as though you're his boss or anything, but still I felt I couldn't let his behavior go unmarked. So I called a meeting with him and made him aware of how very disappointed I was. It was very difficult. In fact, it still is between us."

These are just two examples among hundreds of thousands. We found parish priests who had fashioned their lives around helping others (the theme Belief) but who were also driven to win (the theme Competition). We found marketers who loved ideas (the theme Ideation) but who were equally excited by data and proof (the theme Analytical). We even found writers whose passion for the past (the theme Context) was matched only by their passion for the future (the theme Futuristic). These combinations may be incongruous, but they reflect the reality that individuals cannot easily be squeezed into types. Each of us is unique, sometimes wonderfully so, sometimes infuriatingly so, but always unique. We designed the StrengthsFinder Profile to reveal this uniqueness. In practical terms this means that the possession of one theme will never preclude you from also possessing any other theme.

Can I Develop New Themes if I Don't Like the Ones I Have?

The short answer is no. The StrengthsFinder Profile measures your spontaneous reactions to a series of paired statements. By weaving the reactions together into a pattern, the profile aims to identify the strongest aspects of your mental network, your signature themes. And as we discussed earlier, these signature themes are enduring. No matter how much you might yearn to transform yourself, these themes will prove resistant to change (in test and retest research where we asked three hundred individuals to complete the profile twice, the correlations between the two sets of results was .89; a perfect correlation is 1.0).

Before you lock in on your top five, however, we need to remind you that although your signature themes will not change much during the course of your life, you *can* acquire new knowledge and skills, and these new acquisitions may well lead you into exciting new arenas.

One of the people we interviewed during our research was Danielle J. Guided by such themes such as Empathy and Command, Danielle had carved for herself a successful career as a journalist. Her Empathy enabled her to put her interviewees at ease, while her Command talent made it simple for her to ask the tough questions. For these reasons (and because she could communicate her insights through the written word) she excelled and was promoted to features editor. Then, ten years into her career, she abruptly switched off her word processor and refocused her life. She became a therapist in a hospice.

Journalism, she felt, was interesting but unsatisfying. Prompted by repeated visits to a hospital during her mother's prolonged illness, she reassessed her life and realized that she could make a more significant contribution by joining the ranks of those who helped families deal with the passing of a loved one. So she studied to be a therapist and went to work in her local hospice. Interestingly, though, despite the fact that the knowledge and skills she was now employing were dramatically different, the same dominant themes of Empathy and Command drove her behavior and helped her excel. Her Empathy not only enabled her to discern whether the patient's pain was physical or emotional, but it also guided her to pick just the right words to help the family describe their confusing flood of feelings. To use her word, it enabled her to "join" the family at the right emotional place.

Her Command talent proved even more potent. This was Danielle's description of her use of it in her new role: "When the family has just learned that their loved one is going to die, their overriding feeling is one of shock. They can't believe it. They're angry, confused, and often in denial. The last thing they want in this situation is for someone to goo all over them. Instead, they want someone to take charge. They want someone to tell them what to expect, what to prepare for, and exactly what to do. I found that I was very good at taking control in the way they wanted. I summoned the presence and the clarity they needed."

Danielle serves as one of the thousands of examples of people whose themes remained constant but who nonetheless changed the focus of their lives by acquiring new skills and knowledge. Your life might serve as another example. You might identify with Brian M., a dancer whose love of the stage (the theme Significance) became a love of the theater of the courtroom after he hung up his dancing shoes and took up law. Or you might recognize yourself in Gillian K., a teacher whose desire to help others learn (the theme Developer) found new application in her role as a product support specialist for a pharmaceutical company, where she was paid to educate doctors in the capabilities of new drugs.

Like Danielle, Brian, and Gillian, you might have refocused your life by acquiring new knowledge and skills. If you haven't but feel yourself hemmed in by your signature themes, learn from their example. You may not be able to rewire your brain, but by acquiring new knowledge and skills you *can* redirect your life. You can't develop new themes, but you *can* develop new strengths.

Will I become Too Narrow if I Focus on My Signature Themes?

This is a common question and a legitimate concern. By concentrating on your signature themes you fear you may become so self-involved that you will soon be unable or unwilling to respond to the changing, diverse world around you. You imagine yourself becoming narrow, self-absorbed, a brittle specialist.

If you probe this concern more deeply, however, you will see that your fears are groundless. By focusing on your top five themes you will actually become stronger, more robust, more open to new discoveries and, importantly, more appreciative of people who possess themes very different from your own.

In the course of our research we interviewed many religious leaders. One of them, the prioress of a Benedictine convent, described her philosophy of life this way: "I try to live my life in such a way that when I die and my Maker asks, 'Did you live the life I gave you?' I can honestly answer yes."

No matter what your religious beliefs, the question "Did you live *your* life?" can be quite intimidating. It implies you have a particular life that you are supposed to be living and that any other life is false, inauthentic. Since many of us wander through life plagued by the nagging suspicion that we are making up our life as we go along, we are fearful of even considering this question. And this fear confines us. Unsure of who we really are, we define ourselves by the knowledge we have acquired or the achievements we have racked up along the way. By defining ourselves in this way we become reluctant to change careers or learn new ways of doing things because then, in the new career, we would be forced to jettison our precious haul of expertise and achievement. We would have to jettison our identity.

Furthermore, unsure of who *we* really are, we become reluctant to investigate who *others* really are. Instead, we resort to defining others by their education, their sex, their race, or similarly superficial markers. We take shelter in these generalizations.

Whether in reference to new experiences or new people, our uncertainty about ourselves limits our inquisitiveness about other things. You can avoid this uncertainty. By focusing on your top five themes you can learn who you really are. You can learn that you are not making up your life as you go along. You can learn that your successes and achievements are not accidental. Your signature themes are influencing every single choice you make. Your top five themes explain your successes and achievements. This kind of self-awareness leads to self-confidence. You can face up to that intimidating question "Are you living *your* life?" by answering that no matter what your choice of profession, no matter what the trajectory of your career, if you are applying and refining and polishing your top five themes, then you are indeed living *your* life. You are indeed living the life you were supposed to live. This kind of self-awareness will open you up to be truly inquisitive.

For example, this self-awareness will give you the self-confidence to inquire about a new career. The wonderful quality about themes of talent is that they are transferable from one situation to another. Danielle, the journalist/hospice therapist mentioned in the previous question, could make her dramatic career leap, at least in part, because she knew that her Empathy and Command talents would prove just as powerful in her new role. The same applies to Brian, the dancer/lawyer, and Gillian, the teacher/product specialist. Each of them had to leave behind all the successes and achievements they had acquired in their previous profession, but they brought their top five themes with them. By refining your understanding of your own signature themes you can consider similarly dramatic career shifts or perhaps lateral moves within your organization, sure in the knowledge that you will be bringing your best along with you.

Similarly, this self-awareness will give you the self-confidence to break free from the tyranny of the "shoulds": You "should" become a lawyer or a doctor or a banker because your family expects you to. You "should" accept that next promotion into management because your organization and society at large expects you to. These "shoulds" can assume many forms, but whatever their form, they can create irresistible pressure, and, unfortunately, they are often deaf to the call of your natural talents. The best way to withstand that pressure and strike out in a new, authentic direction is to identify your signature themes of talent. If you want to live a strong life, these themes and the strengths they forge are the only "shoulds" worth listening to.

Finally, by focusing on your distinct themes, you will gain the self-confidence to appreciate the themes of other people. Why? Because the more expert you become in recognizing how your signature themes combine, the more secure you will be in your own uniqueness. Regardless of your race, sex, age, or profession, you will be certain that no one looks at the world in quite the same way you do. And it follows that if you are permanently and wonderfully unique, everyone else must be unique as well. Superficial similarities aside, each person must bring to the world a slightly but meaningfully different perspective. You may relish the challenge of the next mountain to climb (the theme Achiever), but someone else craves to be of service to others (the theme Belief). You may excel at finding patterns in data (the theme Analytical), but another has the vision to see the implications of your discoveries (the theme Futuristic). You may instinctively be able to create a constituency of people who know you and are prepared to go out of their way to help you (the theme Woo), but someone else manages to carve more intimate relationships with these people (the theme Relator).

Counterintuitively, the greater your expertise in the intricacies of your own themes, the more you will be able to identify and then value the intricacies of other people. Conversely, the less respectful you are of your own combination of themes, the less respectful you will be of other people's.

How Can I Manage Around My Weaknesses?

Yes, what about your weaknesses? As we described earlier, many of us are obsessed by our weaknesses. No matter how proud we are of our strengths and no matter how powerful these strengths can sometimes appear, we suspect that our weaknesses are lurking, dragonlike, in the depths of our personality. We hope that by now you have come to realize that your weaknesses are much less imposing—more like gremlins, perhaps, than dragons. If left to their own devices, however, gremlins can still cause their fair share of havoc. Hence, the best advice is not to focus on your strengths and ignore your weaknesses but, rather, to focus on your strengths and find ways to manage your weaknesses. So what is the most effective way to manage a weakness?

To begin with, you need to know what a weakness is. Our definition of a weakness is *anything that gets in the way of excellent performance.* To some this may seem to be an obvious definition, but before skipping past it, bear in mind that it is not the definition of weakness that most of us would use. Most of us would probably side with Webster's and the Oxford English Dictionary and define a weakness as "an area where we lack proficiency." As you strive to build your life around your strengths, we advise you to steer clear of this definition for one very practical reason: Like all of us, you have countless areas where you lack proficiency, but most of them are simply not worth bothering about. Why? Because they don't get in the way of excellent performance. They are irrelevant. They don't need to be managed at all, just ignored.

For example, neither your inability to operate a mass spectrometer nor your ignorance of the sequence of elements in the periodic table are weaknesses because most likely you are not a professional scientist. Unless you are caught short in a game of Trivial Pursuit, you probably couldn't care less that you lack proficiency in these areas.

These are transparent examples in that they refer to specialist knowledge and skills, but what about themes of talent? Surely, if you have low proficiency in a theme such as Strategic, shouldn't we label this a weakness and encourage you to manage around it? Using our definition of weakness the answer is, if you have limited talent for thinking strategically, this is *not* a weakness, any more than not knowing the square root of pi is a weakness. There are hundreds of thousands of roles that don't require you to play "What if?" games and to develop contingency plans, and thus your lack of the Strategic theme is simply a non-talent, an absence. You should ignore it.

But not unlike the gremlins in the film of the same name who were transformed into nasty little critters if they were splashed or if they were fed after midnight, irrelevant non-talents can mutate into real weaknesses under one condition: As soon as you find yourself in a role that *requires* you to play to one of your non-talents—or area of low skills or knowledge—a weakness is born. For example, your ignorance of the stall speed of a Boeing 747, irrelevant most of the time, becomes a devastating weakness if you happen to be piloting one. Likewise, your non-talent for Communication, harmless in your previous role as a research law clerk, swells into a weakness the moment you decide to become a trial lawyer.

So once you know you have a genuine weakness on your hands, a deficiency that actually gets in the way of excellent performance, how can you best deal with it? The first thing you have to do is identify whether the weakness is a skills weakness, a knowledge weakness, or a talent weakness. For example, you might be struggling as a medical device salesperson not because you lack the talent to confront (the theme Command) but because you are wasting your time selling to doctors when the reality of today's healthcare market is that the chief financial officer is the real decision maker.

Or perhaps as a manager your difficulties in delegating effectively have less to do with a stunted Developer theme and more with simply not knowing how to conduct a focused goal-setting session with your employees. In instances such as these, the solution is clear: Go and acquire the skills or knowledge you need.

How can you know for certain that the missing ingredient is knowledge or skill and not talent? Well, since developing excellent performance is hardly an exact science, it's difficult to know for certain, but our advice is this: If, after acquiring the knowledge and skills you feel you need, your performance is still subpar, then by process of elimination the missing ingredient *must* be talent. At which point you should stop wasting time trying to study your way to excellence and, instead, turn to a more creative strategy.

Consider the following five creative strategies, distilled from our interviews with excellent performers, for managing a talent weakness:

1. **Get a little better at it.** This first one doesn't sound very creative, but in a few specific instances it is the only workable strategy. Some activities are baseline requirements for almost any role: being able to communicate your ideas, for example; or listening to others; or organizing your life so that you are where you need to be on any given day; or taking responsibility for your performance. If you do not possess dominant themes in these areas—Communication, Empathy, Discipline, or Responsibility—you will need to hunker down and work to get a little better. For all the reasons we described in previous chapters, you may not enjoy this hunkering, and you will most certainly not reach excellence if this is all you do, but you need to do it nevertheless. Otherwise these weaknesses may well undermine all your great strengths in other areas.

If working to get a little better proves too draining, try the next strategy: Design a simple support system to neutralize your weakness.

2. **Design a support system.** Every morning before Kevin L. puts on his shoes, he takes a moment to imagine himself painting the word "What" on his left shoe and the word "If" on his right. This odd little ritual is his support system for managing around a potentially devastating weakness. Kevin is the national sales manager for a software company, and, rather unsurprisingly, one of his responsibilities is to create the national sales strategy. Kevin brings many talents to this role—he is analytical, creative, impatient—but, unfortunately, the theme Strategic isn't one of them. This means that although he is smart enough to anticipate the obstacles that might derail his plans, his mind doesn't naturally take the time to play out all alternative paths and visualize in detail where they might lead. His early morning shoe scribbling is the best technique he could concoct to remind him to ask the "What if?" questions and so anticipate the obstacles.

During our research these kinds of idiosyncratic support systems kept cropping up. We heard from a congenitally disorganized manager whose support system was the commitment she made to herself that she would always clean out her desk completely once a month. We interviewed another person, a teacher, who was cursed with such a chronically short attention span that she found it virtually impossible to stay focused enough to mark all of her students' papers. Her support system? A rule never to mark more than five papers at a time. Mark five, then get up and make a cup of coffee. Mark another five, then feed the cat.

You probably have your own system that serves as a crutch for one of your persistent talent weaknesses. It might be as straightforward as buying a Palm Pilot to help you keep track of your life or as peculiar as imagining your audience naked in order to calm your nerves before a speech. But whatever it is, don't underestimate its usefulness. You have only a certain amount of time to invest in yourself. A system that stops your worrying about a weakness is freeing up time that can be better spent figuring out how to refine a strength.

Sometimes you don't have to look very far to find the right support system because it can be provided by one of your strong themes. Hence this next strategy.

3. **Use one of your strongest themes to overwhelm your weakness.** Mike K. is a consultant who makes his living giving speeches to business audiences. By all accounts he excels in this role. The fact that he charges thousands per speech and that his dance card is filled for the next twelve months would seem to confirm the judgment that he is an effective public speaker.

No one is more surprised by this turn of events than Mike himself. Twenty years ago if you had told him that he would be speaking to groups of four hundred or five hundred people every week, and entertaining them with his stories and ideas, he would have assumed the worst—that you, like everyone else, were just trying to humiliate him. You see, when Mike was four years old, he developed a stammer. This wasn't one of those occasional under-pressure stammers. It was a constant affliction. Every word was a trap. Those beginning with consonants couldn't even get started. When trying to pronounce them, the impetus to speak would well up inside Mike. He could feel it, but the sound just couldn't seem to push through that first letter. So there he would freeze, a vague noise humming from his mouth, but no word following.

Words beginning with vowels were even worse. The word's first sound would flow easily enough—it was a soft vowel, after all—but then the rest of the word would lag far behind. And so that first vowel sound would repeat itself again and again like a steam engine shunting out of the station but somehow uncoupled from the cars behind.

Needless to say, Mike was mortified by his weakness. He had the misfortune to attend a boarding school in England, and some of his young peers were creatively cruel. His concerned parents dragged him to many a child psychologist in search of a cure, but other than being told to stop straining to compete with his elder brother, Mike learned nothing that could help him. He trudged on through his schooling, dreading the days when he would be asked to read aloud in class, resenting his boisterous schoolmates, and plagued by adolescent fears that he would never marry because he couldn't utter the words "Will you marry me?"

Then one morning a miracle happened. Mike was selected to give a reading to the whole school during morning assembly. On seeing his name on the reading list, Mike was furious. He knew that the school meant no ill will, that they were simply following protocol and assigning one reading to every graduating senior, but, still, what were they thinking? Didn't they know his reading would turn into a freak show? Couldn't they change the protocol and save him the humiliation?

Mike petitioned his principal, but this was England and a boarding school, and, well, no, the protocol couldn't be changed.

The morning of his reading, Mike shuffled toward the lectern, numbed by the magnitude of his impending failure. The night before he had practiced the piece with the principal as his coach, and his stammer had stretched the five-minute piece into a quarter of an hour of suffering. He knew what was about to happen but was powerless to prevent it. Like all tragedies it was inevitable, and so he rounded the lectern, grabbed on to its sides, looked out into the smirking crowd, and took his first breath.

And suddenly, like ambrosia, the words started to flow. They flowed so fast that he could barely keep up with them. They flowed as they were supposed to flow, as words flow for normal people. He found himself in the middle of the piece right on schedule. There was a momentary bobble over the word "sarcasm"—an irony that he appreciates today—and then he was storming through the second half of the piece, easily navigating the minefield words "inevitable" and "multitudes" and "magnificent," gliding toward the finish. He was done. He had read the piece stammer-free. And bizarrely, inconceivably, he had enjoyed it. He looked up to see open mouths, a couple of cheated stares from his schoolyard nemeses, and, wonderful to behold, a dozen or so grins from his closest friends.

They came running up to him afterward: "What happened?" Good question, he thought. After a fruitless decade of therapy focused on fixing his stammer, it had suddenly and very publicly disappeared. What on earth *had* happened?

Thinking back, he realized that just before starting to read, he had looked out over the crowd, seen their faces, and felt . . . energized. Slowly and then with increasing certainty it dawned on him that he loved being onstage—the combination of Significance and Communication, in StrengthsFinder language. The pressure of performing in front of hundreds of people, so frightening to some, was positively uplifting to him. Whereas some people froze in front of crowds, he actually loosened up. His brain seemed to work faster, and the words came more easily. Onstage he was able to do what had always eluded him in real life: He was able to free the thoughts trapped inside his head. He was able to express himself.

Mike took this strength discovery and applied it to his life offstage. Every time he spoke to someone—in the schoolyard, in the car on the way home, on the telephone—he imagined that he was speaking in front of two hundred people. He would picture the scene, see the faces, organize his thoughts carefully, and all of a sudden the words would begin to flow. From that moment on, at college, in his places of employment, with friends and family, he was never again known as "M-M-M-Mike."

Mike stands as an example of the power of strengths to trump weaknesses. After a decade of being defined by his weakness, of desperately trying and failing to fix it, Mike was fortunate to recognize the talents that, properly cultivated, could free him. As you strive to manage around your weaknesses, keep your mind open for the talents that could do the same for you.

4. **Find a partner.** Partnership is one of the lost arts of the corporate world. With job descriptions of the perfect incumbent running to two full pages, and lists of the required competencies growing ever longer, we have become indoctrinated with the notion that an effective employee is a well-rounded employee.

In the face of this indoctrination it is little wonder that so many of us forget that this perfect well-rounded employee is a figment of someone's imagination and that, instead, the "rounding" help we need may well lie in those around us.

By contrast, among the excellent performers we interviewed, we found thousands who had become experts in the art of complementary partnering. They not only could describe their strengths and weaknesses in vivid detail but also identified someone close by whose strengths matched their weaknesses. Some of these weaknesses were knowledge or skills weaknesses, and so the matching strengths were quite easy to spot. We found "numbers-blind" entrepreneurs who had deliberately partnered with "numbers-mad" accountants, and gene-splicing geniuses who had sensibly sought out a legal expert who knew how to secure approval for their miracle drug. However, the most impressive examples were those partnerships built on complementary themes of talent.

There was the senior executive who understood the *concept* that each of his direct reports was different but also realized that he lacked the talent (the theme Individualization) to identify exactly *how* each person was different. Rather than trying to fake it, he hired a human resources professional whose primary role was to help him understand each person's idiosyncracies.

There was the trial lawyer who delivered compelling arguments in the courtroom but detested researching case law in the library (the theme Context). As he built his practice, he knew that his most important recruit would be someone whose passion for researching legal precedent matched his own passion for presentation. He quickly found someone whose eyes lit up at the prospect of long days reading small print, and together they have built a flourishing practice.

Then there was the charming but meek flight attendant who recoiled at the thought of confronting a boisterous passenger or even of giving a pleasant passenger bad news (the theme Command). And so on every flight, before the passengers board, he quietly asks around to see if any of his fellow crew members are good at maintaining their composure when announcing canceled flights, seat mix-ups, or other equally grim tidings. He doesn't always find the perfect partner, but he often does, and to hear him tell it, these partnerships have helped him avoid those situations where in the past he would get flustered, lose his cool, and upset the passenger.

What is impressive about these examples is not the depth of analysis required—in fact, in each of these instances the missing theme(s) was fairly obvious. Rather, what is impressive is simply each person's willingness to admit his imperfection. It takes a strong person to ask for help.

5. **Just stop doing it.** This strategy is a last resort, but when for one reason or another you are forced to try it, you may be surprised by how empowering it can be.

Many of us lose a great deal of time, trust, and respect trying to learn how to do things we simply don't need to do. Why? Because we are encouraged to. Overeager human resources departments insist on defining roles by *how* the work should be done rather than by *what* the work should achieve. They legislate style rather than outcome, thus condemning each employee to learn the desired style. Hence, you find employees who lack the theme Futuristic rehearsing their vision statements because someone has decreed that every employee should have vision. Or you see unfunny managers practicing their jokes in hopes of getting a little wittier because somewhere it is written that "Uses humor appropriately" is a required management competency.

Our interviewees rejected this stylistic conformity. Their advice on how to deal with a particularly persistent weakness? Stop doing it and see whether anyone cares. If you do, they said, three outcomes may surprise you. First, how little anyone cares. Second, how much respect you earn. And third, how much better you feel.

Mary K., a manager who lacked the talent for Empathy, used this strategy. After yet another day of trying and failing to penetrate the mysteries of each person's emotional state, she took a stand. She confessed to each of her employees that she lacked Empathy, saying, "From now on I am not going to try to fake it anymore. I am never going to understand you intuitively, so if you want me to know what you are feeling, you are better off just telling me. And don't think that telling me once at the beginning of the year is enough. How you are feeling is not something that sticks in my memory easily, so you need to keep reminding me; otherwise, I'll never remember."

This confession was met with relief. Her employees knew her to be a basically good person, but it was no surprise to them that she lacked the talent for Empathy. They might have used the word aloof or distant rather than unempathic, but their meaning would have been the same. As one of them said: "Mary is so confused by the world of emotion that she could be your best friend and never know it."

It takes courage, but by confessing her weakness and announcing that she was giving up on it, Mary took a significant step forward as a manager. In the eyes of her employees she became a more authentic person—she was flawed but aware of the flaw—and therefore a more trustworthy manager. Her behavior lost its insincere, "acting" quality and instead became predictable—imperfect, but predictably so. Her employees liked that.

By confessing one of your weaknesses and announcing your intention to give it up, you may net the same outcome. Confess that you have lost the battle with your unfixable weakness, and you may well win the trust and respect of those around you.

Each of these strategies—get a little better at it, design a support system, use one of your strongest themes to overwhelm your weakness, find a partner, and just stop doing it—can help you as you strive to build your life around your strengths. But no matter which strategy you use, never lose your perspective. These strategies do not transform your weaknesses into strengths. They are designed to help you manage around a weakness so that it doesn't get in the way of your strengths. As we have seen, this damage control can be valuable, but on its own it is not enough to lift you to excellence.

One last point on weakness management. Some people wonder if a strong theme can become so dominating that it gets in the way of excellent performance and is thus, by definition, a weakness. For example, can someone have such a powerful Activator theme that he forgets to focus on the future? Or can someone's Command theme be so overwhelming that he frequently upsets the people around him? We have a different view. A person can never have too much of a particular theme. He can only have not enough of another one. For example, rude people don't have too much Command. They have insufficient Empathy. Impatient people don't have too much Activator. They have too little Futuristic talent.

This distinction isn't esoteric. On the contrary, it has practical repercussions. If you assume that the person is struggling to excel because he has too much of a particular theme, then you will tell him to tone the theme down, to stop behaving in that way, and to be less of who he truly is. This is repressive advice. It may be well intentioned, but it is rarely effective. Conversely, if you assume that he is struggling because he has too little of a theme(s), you will offer him more positive advice. You will suggest that he manage around this weakness. You will tell him to decide which of the five strategies would prove most helpful, select one or two of them, and tailor this strategy to his unique situation. This advice often proves challenging to implement, but as advice goes, it is more creative, more purposeful, and thus more effective.

Can My Themes Reveal Whether I Am in the Right Career?

Of all the questions that may keep you up at night as you ponder your career, the two that follow are the most pressing: First, have you chosen the right field for who you are (healthcare, education, mechanical engineering, computer science, fashion, and so on)? Second, are you playing the right role for you? Should you be a salesperson, a manager, an administrator, a writer, a designer, an advisor, an analyst, or some unique combination?

If you choose the right role but the wrong field, you might end up as a natural salesperson selling services you don't believe in or as a genius designer of products that leave you cold. Likewise, honor your passion for a particular field but forget about selecting the right role, and you might find yourself administering schools when you'd rather be teaching in them, or editing newspaper articles instead of writing them.

How can the StrengthsFinder results help you with these two career questions? Your signature themes actually have little to say on the question of which field you should be in, and while they can offer some directional guidance on the subject of role, you would be wise not to take this guidance as gospel.

These answers may surprise you, so take a moment to examine "field" and "role" more closely in order to see precisely where, how, and if StrengthsFinder can help.

FIELD

Have you ever taken one of those career guidance tests, the kind where you respond to a series of questions and learn the field for which you are best suited? These tests are founded on the premise that everyone in a certain field must have a similar disposition. They study your disposition, make a comparison to each field in their database, and then squeeze you into the ones you most closely resemble.

The StrengthsFinder Profile is not one of these tests. StrengthsFinder reveals your signature themes, and while these themes may suggest certain directions your career might take, they do not force you into one field or another. They can't. Why? Quite simply because the research doesn't support a linear relationship between themes and fields. One of the most arresting findings from our interviews was the number of people with similar themes who were excelling in very different fields.

When Jeanne J. and Linda H. completed the StrengthsFinder Profile, three of their top five themes proved to be Significance (a craving for recognized excellence), Activator (a desire for action), and Command (the presence to challenge others). Jeanne and Linda are quite similar in style. They are both assertive, clear, and somewhat intimidating. Their career trajectories are also similar. Both climbed onto the national stage, and, once there, both excelled. But their respective fields couldn't be more different.

Upon finishing graduate school, Jeanne jumped straight into the retail field. She had always loved retail. It was so immediate, so measurable, so direct. The entire process from buying, to merchandising, to customer service fascinated her. She couldn't imagine going into any other field.

In this fast-paced world Jeanne's themes (Activator, Command, and Significance) proved especially powerful. She was never afraid to take action even when, as happened occasionally, she had inadequate information. She never shied away from confronting the people she worked with and challenging them to keep pushing toward outstanding levels of performance. And so up the traditional career ladder she climbed, up through the management ranks of the Disney Stores, up to the presidency of Victoria's Secret, up to the presidency of Banana Republic where she led her team past the $1 billion mark in sales, and onward finally to her current position as president of Wal-Mart's e-business, where she is charged with the challenge of re-creating the world's largest retailer on the Web.

Linda found her field less directly. While studying at the University of Pittsburgh, she met a fellow student who was passionate about law. He was the editor of the campus *Law Review* and spent long hours in the law library preparing articles and layouts for the magazine. Linda didn't have a strong feeling about law one way or the other, but she was (and still is) intrigued by people who are passionate about their work, and so she spent time with him in the library, proofreading the articles and checking the case law. They became friends.

They might have developed their relationship further, but, devastatingly, one week before his graduation he was killed in a car crash while driving home to see his parents. When she could think clearly in those stunned days after the crash, her overriding sense was of things interrupted, cut short. And so, gradually, with little idea of where it would lead, she was moved to pick up his life where he had left it. "It was the most practical thing I could think of to do to honor him," she says now, trying to explain. She enrolled in law school, helped edit the *Law Review,* became as passionate about her studies as he had been, and graduated second in her class.

And then followed a career of firsts. She was the first woman in Texas to clerk for a United States Court of Appeals judge. She was the first woman partner of a major Dallas law firm. She was the first woman to be shortlisted for commissioner of the Securities and Exchange Commission. And having missed that appointment by circumstances beyond her control, she was the first woman to be made chairman of the New York Stock Exchange's legal advisory board.

Linda's natural intelligence obviously had something to do with these achievements, but when you examine her career decisions, you can see that she had more propelling her than a desire to honor the memory of her friend. In fact, at every turn you can see the guiding hand of her signature themes. As the only woman partner in her law firm, she enjoyed the pressure of standing tall, of having to summon the presence to be heard (Command), but she craved a bigger stage (Significance). And so, rather than battering her head on the glass ceiling of the Texas legal community, she deliberately (Activator) cultivated an expertise—the securitization of real estate syndicates—that could give her an independent source of power and credibility. This expertise brought her to the attention of major Wall Street investment banks, which in turn led to significant client relationships, speaking engagements, authoring books, and visiting professorships, thereby catapulting her out of Texas and onto the national scene.

Jeanne's and Linda's stories reveal that there are many ways to find the right field. Jeanne felt hers in her bones. Linda fell into hers to honor a friend (and incidentally, today, despite her success, she thinks that if she had to do it over again, she would probably choose entrepreneurship, not law, as her field). You will need to find your field in the same way—by listening to the yearnings that pull you and then seeing what moves you. If you don't feel a strong pull, you will need to experiment in school or in your first years in the working world and narrow your focus by elimination.

That is why we said that StrengthsFinder doesn't serve to funnel you into a particular field. In their search for the right field, neither Jeanne nor Linda would have been helped by knowing their signature themes because, despite their different fields, their themes were very similar. The same applies to you. Your signature themes will not necessarily help you choose between being a retailer, a lawyer, or even a carpenter. What they *can* help you do is make the most of whatever field you choose.

ROLE

The StrengthsFinder Profile has more to offer you here. From our research it is apparent that people who excel in the same role do possess some similar themes. For example, many of the journalists we interviewed found that the theme Adaptability was in their top five. From one day to the next they never know where their work might take them. On Monday evening they might find themselves huddling in the rain outside the Ramada Inn at Newark Airport waiting to interview plane crash survivors, and on Tuesday morning they are back at the office finishing up an article on the impact of rising interest rates. Whereas some of us would feel mental whiplash at these constant changes of subject, tone, and location, people blessed with Adaptability feel energized. They feed on the unexpected.

Many of the doctors in our study, no matter what their specialty, possessed the theme Restorative. Every day they are faced with patients in need of help. They must respond to each person's present need, knowing that no matter how diligently and caringly they apply themselves, the future will only bring them more sick people to heal. This would be an endless, thankless role if they weren't guided by the talent to derive deep satisfaction from a patient's recovery or, in some cases, by a patient's growing acceptance of his own passing.

In the same vein we found thousands of teachers with themes such as Developer, Empathy, and Individualization who presumably used these talents to great effect in helping each student learn. Command, Activator, and Competition were talents frequently found in the top five of the salespeople we interviewed, enabling them to thrill to the challenge of confrontation and persuasion, and to the opportunity to measure their effectiveness against their peers.

Despite these discoveries, however, you need to be careful about drawing too straight a line between a particular theme and a particular role. We suggest caution because our research interviews indicate that thousands of people with very different theme combinations nonetheless play the same role equally well.

Steve S. and Victoria S. are both successful entrepreneurs, and yet Steve's top five are Competition, Analytical, Strategic, Ideation, and Futuristic, whereas Victoria's are Empathy, Developer, Restorative, Context, and Consistency. With these very different theme combinations, how can they excel in a similar role? They do it by crafting their role to fit their signature themes.

Steve runs an Internet company called Icebox that produces and distributes cartoon shorts on the Web. His particular genius lies in being able to persuade film directors and venture capitalists to see and literally buy into his vision of the future. His business model is incomplete, his content (at the time of writing) is still inside his directors' heads, and the technology for streaming video is a couple of years from full functionality. And yet he revels in the challenge of weaving this uncertainty into a compelling picture of a profitable business. He has assembled a team of competent executors and people managers, leaving him free to do what he loves.

Victoria runs a twelve-year-old $7 million London-based public relations firm that specializes in full-service hotel chains such as Four Seasons and Swissôtel. By her own admission she is not a business strategist, preferring to hand off those duties to her ex-banker partner. Instead, Victoria concerns herself with managing the operations side of the business. She is the one who selects new associates, positions them on the appropriate accounts, figures out what each one needs to learn, and listens to their problems. In this role she gets to use most, if not all, of her top five themes, and as a result her business and the forty employees within it are thriving.

Steve would fail miserably in Victoria's role. Victoria would recoil from Steve's. Yet both excel in entrepreneurship.

John F. flies Boeing 737's for American Airlines. Gilles R. flies 767's for Air France. John's top five are Consistency, Harmony, Context, Developer, and Relator. Gilles's are Consistency, Harmony, Discipline, Responsibility, and Learner. They have Consistency and Harmony in common. When you think about it, that makes some sense given the responsibilities of an airline captain. The Consistency theme prompts them to treat each passenger equally and to strictly enforce all the safety rules, no matter how uppity a certain frequent-flying passenger may become. Their Harmony theme ensures that they look for common ground in the cockpit, and if a disagreement does occur, it is quickly smoothed over so that pilot and copilot can get on with the business of flying the plane.

But what about the rest of their themes? How do they play out? John's Developer, Context, and Relator themes have pushed him in a very particular direction. He has become a teacher. His actual title is Captain Check Airman, Instructor Type, but in layman's parlance he is a teacher. He trains crews in how to operate the new Boeing 737-800. In this role he not only gets to flex his Relator and Developer muscles as he builds relationships with his students and strives to help them learn but he also uses his Context theme to good effect. Apparently, the best training method for pilots is the case method. This is how John describes it: "Every two weeks I have a hundred pilots in here, and I basically talk about how to maneuver the airplane in situations they might find themselves in. I just draw on numerous stories of others who were less fortunate in their recoveries and tell them how to do it better. Pilots are big on the past and on history because that's how we learn, that's how we move forward."

Gilles's three remaining themes, Discipline, Responsibility, and Learner, have found a different outlet. Gilles loves to fly. To be more precise, Gilles loves to land. He knows that as the captain he is responsible for the safe passage of the passengers on board, so on every flight he takes pride in paying attention to every detail, particularly the landing. For him there is no feeling quite like putting the plane down so perfectly that the passengers barely notice that the wheels have touched the ground. He rarely receives thanks for this precision performance, but *he* knows that, in pilotspeak, he's "greased one in."

This explains how his Responsibility and Discipline themes are expressed. What about his Learner theme? It turns out that other than enjoying the intricate details of learning to fly, Gilles hasn't directed this theme toward his actual work. Instead, he has relied on it to fill his long layover hours. He reads all the time. He has become a proficient pianist and pipe organist. He has learned German and Spanish. Why? "No reason, really. I don't necessarily learn things to use to my advantage. I just learn things because I like studying. I like acquiring new skills."

Each of these examples reminds us that no matter what the role, there are many routes to excellence. Yes, some themes seem to fit certain roles. But, no, you shouldn't necessarily decide that you are miscast just because some of your themes do not at first glance match your role.

Our research into human strengths does not support the extreme, and extremely misleading, assertion that "you can play any role you set your mind to," but it does lead us to this truth: Whatever you set your mind to, *you will be most successful when you craft your role to play to your signature talents most of the time.* We hope that by highlighting your signature themes we can help you craft such a role.

CHAPTER 6

Managing Strengths

- "FIDEL," SAM MENDES, AND PHIL JACKSON

- ONE BY ONE

"Fidel," Sam Mendes, and Phil Jackson

"What is the secret of their success?"

There are many things you can do to avoid failing as a manager. You can set clear expectations. You can highlight the underlying purpose of people's work. You can correct people when they do something wrong. And you can praise people when they do something right. If you do all these things often and well, you will not fail as a manager.

However, neither will you necessarily succeed. To excel as a manager, to turn your people's talents into productive powerful strengths, requires an additional, all-important ingredient. Lacking this ingredient, no matter how diligently you set expectations, communicate purpose, correct mistakes, or praise good performance, you will never reach excellence. The all-important ingredient is *Individualization,* and this is what it sounds like:

Ralph Gonzalez works as store manager for Best Buy, the phenomenally successful consumer electronic retailer. A couple of years ago he was charged with resurrecting a troubled store in Hialeah, Florida, and with his passion, his creativity, and his slightly disconcerting resemblance to a youthful Fidel Castro, he made an immediate impression. To give his people an identity and a purpose he named his store The Revolution and dubbed each one of them a revolutionary (a particularly daring decision given the anti-Castro sentiment in south Florida, and yet it worked). He drafted a Declaration of Revolution and required that certain project teams wear army fatigues. He posted all the relevant performance numbers in the break room and deliberately overcelebrated every small improvement. And to drive home the point that excellence is everywhere, he gave all employees a whistle and told them to blow it loudly whenever they saw any employee or supervisor or manager do something "revolutionary." Today the whistles come so frequently that they drown out the Bob Marley CD playing over the loudspeakers, and the store's numbers confirm the whistling: No matter which number one uses—sales growth, profit growth, customer satisfaction, or employee retention—the Hialeah store is one of Best Buy's best.

But, surprisingly, when interviewed, Ralph didn't attribute his success to The Revolution, to the whistles, or even to his likeness to a young Castro. Instead, he said this: "Everything comes down to knowing your people. I always start by asking each new employee, 'Are you a people person or a box person?' In other words, is this person drawn to strike up a conversation with our customers, or does he love arranging the merchandise so that each product looks as if it's about to jump off the shelf? If he is a people person, I will keep watching to see whether he is just a natural smiler, in which case I'll probably put him on a checkout register or in customer service, or whether he also has the talent to sell, in which case I'll set him up to give multiple presentations of our newer, more complicated products during our busiest times. And then I'll watch to see how he likes to be managed. Right now I have a merchandise manager who needs me to be firm and challenging; he's that kind of guy, and he expects the same from me. But I also have an inventory manager who needs something very different from me. He wants me to explain myself very clearly and to talk about exactly *why* we need to do something. I keep watching like this, getting to know each of them. If I didn't, none of the other stuff would work."

Ralph Gonzalez, toiling away in relative obscurity in south Florida, is only one of the great managers who have founded their approach on the concept of individualization. During our interviews we discovered tens of thousands like him in factories, sales departments, hospital wards, and boardrooms. In fact, no matter where we looked, no matter how anonymous or glamorous the environment, when we studied great managers, they all seemed to share this passion for individualization.

When Sam Mendes, the young Oscar-winning director of the film *American Beauty,* was asked by the British newspaper the *Independent* to describe the secret of his success, he said, "I am not a master-class director. I am not a teacher. I am a coach. I don't have a methodology. Each actor is different. And on the film set you have to be next to them all, touching them on the shoulder, saying, 'I'm with you. I know exactly how you're working.' . . . Kevin Spacey likes to joke and . . . do impersonations right up to the moment of action, on his mobile phone to his agent or whatever. The more relaxed, the more jovial he is, the more he's not thinking about what he does. When you say, 'Action,' he's like a laser beam. His relaxation leads to spontaneity. So to Kevin you're saying, 'Give me a Walter Matthau impersonation.' Annette Bening, on the other hand, is on her Walkman half an hour before the cameras roll, cutting off the set, focused down, listening to the music that the character would listen to. . . . All I know is that I operate by going out to each of them and trying to learn the territory in which they operate." He summed up: "My language to each of them has to suit their brain."

When Phil Jackson, the coach of the six-time NBA championship–winning Chicago Bulls, went to the L.A. Lakers, he brought with him all of the techniques that had served him so well in Chicago, the Zen philosophy, the meditation sessions, the triangle offensive system. But he also brought books—a different book, it turned out, for each player. To the young superstar Kobe Bryant he gave a copy of *The White Boy Shuffle* by Paul Beatty because he felt that the story—of a black boy raised in a predominantly white community—reflected the challenges of Kobe's own upbringing in suburban Philadelphia. To Shaquille O'Neal, one of the most recognized and celebrated basketball players in the world, he chose Friedrich Nietzsche's autobiography *Ecce Homo* because it dealt with the subject of a man's search for identity, prestige, and power. Rick Fox, who is said to have aspirations as an actor, received a copy of the noted Hollywood director Elia Kazan's autobiography.

Why select different books for each player? According to Jackson, "The books are to show that I appreciate them and am focused on who they are."

In your role as manager you have the same opportunity. You will need to focus on who each employee is. You will need to learn each one's behavior and, as Sam Mendes did, find the right language "to suit their brain." The expectations you set will be slightly different for each person. The way you set them will also be different for each, as will the way you talk about your company's mission, the way you correct a mistake, the way you nurture a strength, and the way you praise, what you praise, and why. All your moves as a manager will need to be tailored to each individual employee.

Daunting though this may sound, there is no getting around it. Each employee is wired just a little bit differently. If you are to keep your talented employees and spur each of them on to greater performance, you will have to discern how each one is unique and then figure out ways to capitalize on this uniqueness.

For a couple of reasons this often proves difficult to do. The first reason is that the great majority of organizations, with their formalized processes and their detailed lists of competencies, operate under the assumption that most employees are the same and that, if not, they should be retrained until they are. The manager who individualizes will invariably butt heads within such organizations.

Second, it is hard because individualizing your management style is more time-consuming than treating all employees the same. Faced with many other responsibilities, it would have been so much simpler for Ralph, Sam, and Phil to ignore each employee's pattern and say, in essence, "Look, this is the way I manage. If you like it, good. If not, either adapt or go somewhere else." None of them did, but with spans of control in some organizations stretching one manager to thirty, forty, or even fifty employees, you can hardly blame the managers that take the easier route.

We cannot help you very much with the first reason, short of suggesting that you ask your organization's leaders to read the next chapter. If you are trapped in an organization that tries to train employees in the same role to acquire exactly the same style, your attempts to individualize will always meet resistance. However, we can address the second reason, lack of time. Let's explore a few ideas about how to manage individuals with different signature themes.

One By One

"How can you manage each of the thirty-four themes of StrengthsFinder?"

They say that if you really want to know how to work with some-one, you should play a round of golf with him. This notion may have some merit, but it is not the most practical advice. Some of us despise the game, and those of us who love it do not always have eighteen holes available when we need them. Besides, there are other, less time-consuming ways to investigate the details of each person's strengths.

As a manager, once you know the top five themes of each of your employees, you can read through the suggestions in the following pages for each particular theme. Select a few that seem especially relevant for each employee. When appropriate, discuss your selections with the employee. Refine them together. And gradually, one employee at a time, you may find yourself conjuring the same kind of near perfect performances enjoyed by the likes of Ralph Gonzalez, Sam Mendes, and Phil Jackson.

Of course, nothing can replace the insights you gain from simply spending time with each employee, particularly if you possess the theme Individualization. And no idea will work if your people don't trust your intentions toward them. However, if your challenge is not lack of trust but lack of time, these suggestions may prove helpful.

HOW TO MANAGE A PERSON STRONG IN ACHIEVER

- When there are times that require extra work, call on this person. Remember that the saying "If you want to get a job done, ask a busy person" is generally true.

- Recognize that he likes to be busy. Sitting in meetings is likely to be very boring for him. So either let him get his work done or arrange to have him attend only those meetings where you really need him and he can be fully engaged.

- Help him measure what he gets done. He may well enjoy keeping track of hours, but, more important, he should have a way to measure cumulative production. Simple measures such as number of customers served, customers known by name, files reviewed, prospects contacted, or patients seen will help give him definition.

- Establish a relationship with this person by working alongside him. Working hard together is often a bonding experience for him. And keep low producers away from him. "Slackers" annoy him.

- When this person finishes a job, a rest or an easy assignment is rarely the reward he wants. He will be much more motivated if you give recognition for past achievement and then a new goal that stretches him.

- This person may well need less sleep and get up earlier than most. Look to him when these conditions are required on the job. Also, ask him questions such as "How late did you have to work to get this done?" or "When did you come in this morning?" He will appreciate this kind of attention.

- You may be tempted to promote him to higher-level roles simply because he is a self-starter. This may be a mistake if it leads him away from what he does best. A better course would be to pinpoint his other themes and strengths, and look for opportunities for him to do more of what he does well.

HOW TO MANAGE A PERSON STRONG IN ACTIVATOR

- Ask this person what new goals or improvements should be achieved by your division. Select an area that fits and give her the responsibility for initiating and organizing the project.

- Let her know that you know she is a person who can make things happen and that you will be asking her for help at key times. Your expectations will energize her.

- Assign her to a team that is bogged down and talks more than it performs. She will stir them into action.

- When this person complains, listen carefully—you may learn something. But then get her on your side by talking about new initiatives that she can lead or new improvements she can make tomorrow. Do this quickly because, unchecked, she can quickly stir up negativity when she gets offtrack.

- Examine her other dominant themes. If she is strong in the Command talent, she may have the potential to sell and persuade very effectively. If she is also strong in Relator or Woo, she may become an excellent recruiter for you, drawing in the recruit and then pressing him to commit.

- To prevent her from running into too many obstacles, partner her with people strong in Strategic or Analytical talent. They can help her look around the corner. However, you may have to intercede for her in these partnerships so that her instinct to act is not stymied by their desire to project and analyze.

HOW TO MANAGE A PERSON STRONG IN ADAPTABILITY

- This person lives to react and respond. Position him so that his success depends on his ability to accommodate the unforeseen and then run with it.

- Let him know about the planning you are doing, but unless he is also strong in Focus, don't expect him to do the planning with you. He is likely to find much planning work endlessly boring.

- With his instinctively flexible nature he is a valuable addition to almost every team. When balls are dropped or plans go awry, he will adjust to the new circumstances and try to make progress. He will not sit on the sidelines and sulk.

- He will be most productive on short-term assignments that require immediate action. He prefers a life filled with many quick skirmishes rather than long, drawn-out campaigns.

- Examine his other dominant themes. If he also has a talent for Empathy, you might try positioning him where he has to be sensitive to and accommodate the varied needs of customers or guests. If one of his other strong themes is Developer, you should cast him in a mentor role. With his willingness to "go with the flow" he can provide a wonderful environment in which others can experiment and learn.

- Be ready to excuse this person from meetings about the future, such as goal-setting meetings or career-counseling sessions. He is a "here-and-now" person and so will find these meetings rather irrelevant.

HOW TO MANAGE A PERSON
STRONG IN ANALYTICAL

- Whenever this person is involved with an important decision, take time to think through the issues with her. She will want to know all the factors affecting the decision.

- If you are explaining a decision that has already been made, always remember to lay out the logic of the decision very clearly. To you it may feel as though you are overexplaining things, but for her this level of detail is essential if she is to commit to the decision.

- Every time you have the opportunity, recognize and praise her reasoning ability. She is proud of her disciplined mind.

- When defending a decision or a principle, show this person the supporting numbers. She instinctively gives more credibility to information that displays numbers.

- Remember that she has a need for *exact, well-researched* numbers. Never try to pass shoddy data to her as credible evidence.

- A highlight in her life is to discover patterns in data. Always give her the opportunity to explain the pattern in detail to you. This will be motivational for her and will help to solidify your relationship.

- You will not always agree with her, but always take her point of view seriously. She has probably thought through her points very carefully.

- Because the accuracy of the work is so important to her, getting a task done correctly may be more important to her than meeting a deadline. Therefore, as the deadline draws near, keep checking in with her to ensure that she has the necessary time to do it right.

HOW TO MANAGE A PERSON STRONG IN ARRANGER

- This person will thrive on responsibility, so give him as much as you are able, according to his knowledge and skill levels.

- He may well have the talent to be a manager or supervisor. His Arranger theme enables him to figure out how people with very different strengths can work together.

- When you are launching a project, give him the opportunity to choose and position the members of the project team. He is good at figuring out how each person's strengths might add greatest value to the team.

- He is excited by complex, multifaceted assignments. He will thrive in situations where he has many things going on at the same time.

- He can be resourceful. Feel confident that you can slot him into a role where something is not working, and he will enjoy figuring out other ways of doing things.

- Pay attention to his other strong themes. If he also has talent for Discipline, he may be an excellent organizer, establishing routines and systems for getting things done.

- Understand that his modus operandi for team building is through trust and relationship. He may well reject someone who he believes is dishonest or does shoddy work.

HOW TO MANAGE A PERSON STRONG IN BELIEF

- This person will have a passion about something. Discover her passion and tie it to the work to be done.

- She will have some powerful permanent values. Figure out how to align her values with those of the organization. For example, talk with her about how your products and services make the lives of people better, or discuss how your company embodies integrity and trust, or give her opportunities to go above and beyond to help colleagues and customers. In this way, through her actions and words, she will make visible the values of your organization's culture.

- Learn about her family and community. She will have made rock solid commitments here. You will need to understand, appreciate, and honor these commitments, and she will respect you for it.

- Realize that she may place more value on opportunities to provide greater levels of service than on opportunities to make more money. Find ways to enhance this natural service orientation, and you will see her at her best.

- You do not have to share this person's belief system, but you do have to understand it, respect it, and apply it. If you cannot apply her values to either your goals or your organization's, you should perhaps help her find a different work situation. Otherwise, major conflicts will eventually erupt.

HOW TO MANAGE A PERSON STRONG IN COMMAND

- When you need to jar a project loose and get things moving again or when people need to be persuaded, ask this person to take charge.

- Always ask him for evaluations of what is happening in your organization. He is most likely to give you a straight answer. In the same vein, look to him to raise ideas different from your own. He isn't likely to be a head nodder.

- As much as you can, give him the room to lead and make decisions. He will not like to be supervised closely.

- If he starts empire building, upsetting colleagues, veering from focus, or ignoring his commitments, meet him head-on. Confront him directly with specific examples. Take firm action and, if necessary, require immediate restitution. Then arrange for him to be productive as soon as possible. He will get over his mistake quickly, and so should you.

- Never threaten him unless you are 100 percent ready to follow through.

- This person may intimidate others with his up-front, assertive style. You may need to weigh whether or not the contribution of this person who makes things happen justifies the occasional ruffled feather. Rather than pushing him to learn how to be empathic and polite, your time may be better spent helping his colleagues understand that his assertiveness is part of what makes him effective—as long as he remains assertive rather than aggressive or offensive.

HOW TO MANAGE A PERSON STRONG IN COMMUNICATION

- Explore with this person how her communication strengths can be developed so she can make an even more significant contribution to the organization.

- She finds it easy to carry on a conversation. Ask her to come to social gatherings, dinners, or any events where you want to entertain prospects or customers.

- Ask her to learn the folklore, the stories of interesting events within your organization, and then give her the opportunity to tell these stories to her colleagues. She will help bring your culture to life, and thereby strengthen it.

- Take the time to hear about her life and experiences. She will enjoy the telling. You will enjoy the listening. And your relationship will be closer because of it.

- Discuss your plans with her for your organization's social events. She is likely to have good ideas both for entertainment and for what should be communicated at the event.

- Ask her to help some of the specialists in your organization make more engaging presentations. In some situations she should actually make the presentation for the specialist.

- If you send her to public speaking training, make sure to place her in a small class with advanced students and a top-level trainer. She will quickly chafe in a remedial beginners class.

HOW TO MANAGE A PERSON STRONG IN COMPETITION

- Use competitive language with this person. For example, it is a win-lose world for this person, so from his perspective, achieving a goal is winning and missing a goal is losing. When you need to engage him in planning or problem solving, use the competitive word "outsmart."

- Measure him against other people, particularly other competitive people. You may decide to post the performance records of all your people, but remember that only your competitive people will get a kick out of this public comparison. Others may resent it and be mortified by the comparison.

- Set up contests for him. Pit him against other competitors even if you have to find competitors in business units other than your own. Highly charged competitors want to compete with others who are very close to their skill level. Matching them against modest achievers will not motivate them.

- Find places where he can win. If he loses repeatedly, he may stop playing. Remember, in the contests that matter to him, he doesn't compete for the fun of competing. He competes to win.

- Consider that one of the best ways to manage him is to hire another competitive person who produces more.

- Talk about talents with him. Like all competitors he knows that it takes talent to be a winner. Name his talents. Tell him that he needs to marshal his talents to win. Do not "Peter Principle" this person by suggesting that "winning" means getting promoted. Help him focus on winning where his true talents lie.

- When this person loses, he may need to mourn for a while. Let him. Then quickly move him into another opportunity to win.

HOW TO MANAGE A PERSON STRONG IN CONNECTEDNESS

- This person will likely have social issues that she will defend strongly. Listen closely to know what these issues are. Your acceptance of these issues will influence the depth of relationship you can build with her.

- She is likely to have a spiritual orientation and perhaps a strong faith. Your knowledge and, at the very least, acceptance of her spiritual position will enable her to become increasingly comfortable around you.

- Encourage this person to build bridges to the different groups in your organization. She naturally thinks about how things are connected, so she should excel at showing different people how each relies on the others. Properly positioned, she can be a team builder in your company.

- She may be very receptive to thinking about and developing the mission for your organization. She likes to feel part of something larger than herself.

- If you are also strong in Connectedness, share articles, writings, and experiences with her. You can reinforce each other's focus.

HOW TO MANAGE A PERSON STRONG IN CONSISTENCY

- When it comes time to recognize the team after the completion of a project, ask this person to pinpoint each person's contribution. She will ensure that each person receives the accolades he or she truly deserves.

- When you need to put consistent practices in place, ask her to help establish the routine ways of doing things for your organization.

- Be supportive of her during times of great change because she is most comfortable with predictable patterns that she knows work well.

- When in an analytical role, ask this person to work on group data rather than individual data. She is likely to be more adept at discovering generalizations that can be made about the group rather than particulars about a certain individual.

- If as a manager you struggle with situations where rules must be applied equally and absolutely and no favoritism must be shown, ask her to step in and deal with them. The explanations and justifications will come naturally to her.

- In those situations where it is necessary to treat diverse people equally, ask her to contribute to the development of the rules.

- She has a practical bent and thus will tend to prefer getting tasks accomplished and decisions made rather than more abstract work such as brainstorming or long-range planning.

HOW TO MANAGE A PERSON STRONG IN CONTEXT

- When you ask this person to do something, take time to explain the thinking that led to this action. He needs to understand the background for a course of action before he can commit to it.

- When you introduce him to new colleagues, ask these colleagues to talk about their background before you all get down to business.

- During meetings always turn to him to review what has been done and what has been learned up to the present time. Instinctively, he will want others to be aware of the context of decision-making.

- He thinks in terms of case studies, that is, when did we meet a similar situation, what did we do, what happened, what did we learn? You can expect him to use this talent to help others learn, especially when the need for case studies is important. No matter what the subject matter, ask him to collect revealing anecdotes, to highlight the key discovery from each anecdote, and perhaps to build a class around these case studies.

- He can do the same in relation to your organization's culture. Ask him to collect anecdotes of people behaving in a way that exemplifies the cornerstones of the culture. His anecdotes, retold in newsletters, training classes, Web sites, videos, and so on, will strengthen your culture.

HOW TO MANAGE A PERSON
STRONG IN DELIBERATIVE

- Do not position this person in a role that requires snap judgments. She is likely to feel uncomfortable making decisions on gut alone.

- Ask her to join teams or groups that tend to be impulsive. She will have a temporizing effect, adding much-needed thoughtfulness and anticipation to the mix.

- She is likely to be a rigorous thinker. Before you make a decision, ask her to help you identify the land mines that may derail your plans.

- In situations where caution is required, such as situations that are sensitive to legal, safety, or accuracy issues, ask her to take the lead. She will instinctively anticipate where the dangers might lie and how to keep your flanks protected.

- She is likely to excel at negotiating contracts, especially behind the scenes. As far as you can within the confines of her job description, ask her to play this role.

- Honor that she may be quite a private person. Unless invited, do not push to become too familiar with her too quickly. And by the same token, do not take it personally if she keeps you at arm's length.

- Do not ask her to be a greeter, rainmaker, or networker for your organization. The kind of effusiveness that this role requires may not be in her repertoire.

- In her relationships she will be selective and discriminating. Consequently, do not move her quickly from team to team. She needs to be confident that the people she surrounds herself with are competent and can be trusted, and this confidence takes time to build.

- As a manager she will be known as someone who gives praise sparingly, but when she does, it is truly deserved.

HOW TO MANAGE A PERSON STRONG IN DEVELOPER

- Ask this person to tell you which associates are growing in their jobs. He is likely to pick up small increments of growth that others miss.

- Position him so that he can help others within the organization grow. For example, give him the opportunity to mentor one or two people of his choice or to teach a class on a company topic, such as safety, benefits, or customer service.

- Be prepared to pay the fee for him to belong to a local training organization.

- Set him up as the one who will give recognition to colleagues. He will enjoy selecting the achievements that deserve praise, and his colleagues on the receiving end will know that the praise is genuine.

- He may be a candidate for a supervisor, team leader, or manager role.

- If he is already a manager or executive, look to his business unit for people who can be transferred to positions with larger responsibilities in the organization. He grows people and prepares them for the future.

- Reinforce his self-concept as a person who encourages people to stretch and to excel. For example, tell him, "They would never have broken the record by themselves. Your encouragement and confidence gave them the spark they needed."

- Be aware that he may protect a struggling performer long past the time when she should have been moved or terminated. Help him focus his developing instincts on setting people up to achieve success, and not on supporting people who are enduring hardship. The most developmental action he can take with a person enduring hardship is to find her a different opportunity where she can truly excel.

HOW TO MANAGE A PERSON
STRONG IN DISCIPLINE

- Give this person the opportunity to bring structure to a haphazard or chaotic situation. Since she will never be comfortable in such shapeless, messy situations—and don't expect her to—she will not rest until order and predictability are restored.

- Clutter will annoy her. Don't expect her to last long in a physically cluttered environment. Either charge her with cleaning it up or find her a different environment.

- Always give her advance notice of deadlines. She feels a need to get work done ahead of schedule, and she can't do this if you don't tell her the schedule.

- In the same vein, try not to surprise her with sudden changes in plan and priority. Surprises are distressing to her. They can ruin her day.

- When there are many things that need to get done in a set time period, remember her need to prioritize. Take the time to prioritize together and then, once the schedule is set, stick to it.

- If appropriate, ask her to help you plan and organize your own work. You might ask her to review your time management system or even your proposal for reengineering some of your department's processes. Tell her colleagues that this is one of her strengths and encourage them to ask her for similar help.

- She excels at developing routines that help her work efficiently. If she is forced to work in a situation that requires flexibility and responsiveness, encourage her to devise a set number of routines, each appropriate for a certain situation. In this way she will have a predictable response to fall back on, no matter what the surprise.

HOW TO MANAGE A PERSON STRONG IN EMPATHY

- Ask this person to help you know how certain people within your organization are feeling. He is sensitive to the emotions of others.

- Before securing his commitment to a particular course of action, ask him how he feels and how other people feel about the issues involved. For him, emotions are as real as other, more practical factors and must be weighed when making decisions.

- Pay attention but do not overreact when he cries. Tears are part of his life. He may sense the joy or tragedy in another person's life more poignantly than even that person does.

- Help this person to see his Empathy as a special gift. It may come so naturally to him that he now thinks everyone feels what he feels, or he may be embarrassed by his strength of feeling. Show him how to use it to everyone's advantage.

- Test this person's ability to make decisions instinctively rather than logically. He may not be able to articulate why he thinks that a certain action is right, but he will often be right nonetheless. Ask him, "What is your gut feeling about what we should do?"

- Arrange for him to work with positive, optimistic people. He will pick up on these feelings and be motivated. Conversely, steer him away from pessimists and cynics. They will depress him.

- When employees or customers have difficulty understanding why an action is necessary, ask him for help. He may be able to sense what they are missing.

HOW TO MANAGE A PERSON STRONG IN FOCUS

- Set goals with timelines and then let this person figure out how to achieve them. He will work best in an environment where he can control his work events.

- Check in with him on a regular basis, as often as he indicates would be helpful. He will thrive on these regular check-ins because he likes talking about goals and his progress toward them. Ask him how often you should meet to discuss goals and objectives.

- Do not always expect him to be sensitive to the feelings of others because getting his work done often takes priority over feelings. If he also possesses a talent for Empathy, this effect will obviously be lessened. Nonetheless, always be aware of the possibility that he may trample on feelings as he marches toward his goal.

- He does not revel in situations of constant change. To manage this, use language that he can understand when describing the change. For example, talk about change in terms of "new goals" and "new measures of success." Terms like this give the change trajectory and purpose. This is the way he naturally thinks.

- When there are projects with critical deadlines, ask him to get involved. He instinctively honors deadlines. As soon as he comes to own a project with a deadline, he will concentrate all his energies on it until it is completed.

- Arrange for him to attend a time management seminar. He may not naturally excel at this, but because his Focus theme pushes him to move toward his goals as fast as possible, he will appreciate the greater efficiency that time management brings.

- Be aware that unstructured meetings will bother him, so when he is in a meeting, try to follow the agenda.

HOW TO MANAGE A PERSON STRONG IN FUTURISTIC

- When you have career conferences or performance meetings with this person, keep in mind that she lives for the future. Ask her to share her vision with you—her vision about her career, about your organization, and about the marketplace/field in general.

- Give her time to think, write about, and plan for the products and services needed in the future. Carve out opportunities for her to share her perspective in company newsletters, meetings, or industry conventions.

- Send her any data or articles you spot that would be of interest to her. She needs grist for her futuristic mill.

- Put her on the organization's planning committee. Have her present her data-based vision of what the organization might look like three years hence. Have her repeat this presentation every six months or so. In this way she can refine it with new data and insight.

- Stimulate her by talking with her often about what could be. Ask lots of questions. Push her to make the future she sees as vivid as possible.

- When the organization needs its people to embrace change, ask her to put these changes in the context of the organization's future needs. Have her make a presentation or write an internal article that puts these changes in perspective. She can help others rise above their present uncertainties and become almost as excited as she is about the possibilities of the future.

HOW TO MANAGE A PERSON STRONG IN HARMONY

- As far as possible steer this person away from conflict. Do not include him in meetings where there will almost certainly be conflict because he is not at his best when confronting others.

- Determine in what ways you agree with him and regularly review these agreements with him. Surround him with other people strong in Harmony. He will always be more focused, more productive, and more creative when he knows that he is supported.

- Don't waste your time discussing controversial subjects with this person. He will not enjoy the debate for its own sake. Instead, keep your discussions focused on practical matters where clear action can be taken.

- Don't always expect him to disagree with you even when you are wrong. For the sake of harmony he may nod his head despite judging your idea a poor one. Consequently, you may need other people who instinctively voice their opinions to help keep your thinking clear.

- Sometimes when others are locked in disagreement, he can unlock them. He will not necessarily resolve the subject under debate, but he will help them find other areas where they do agree. These areas of common ground can be the starting point for working productively together again.

- He wants to feel sure about what he is doing. Help him find authoritative backup (expert opinion) for the actions he takes.

HOW TO MANAGE A PERSON STRONG IN IDEATION

- This person has creative ideas. Be sure to position her where her ideas will be valued.

- She will be particularly effective as a designer, whether of sales strategies, marketing campaigns, customer service solutions, or new products. Whatever her field, try to make the most of her ability to design.

- Since she thrives on ideas, try to feed her new ideas that lie within the focus of your organization. She will not only be more excited about her work but will also use these ideas to generate new insights and discoveries of her own.

- Encourage her to think of useful ideas or insights that can be shared with your best customers. From Gallup's research it is clear that when a company deliberately teaches its customers something, their level of loyalty increases.

- She enjoys the power of words. Whenever you come across a word combination that perfectly captures a concept, idea, or pattern, share it with her. It will stimulate her thinking.

- She needs to know that everything fits together. When decisions are made, take time to show her how each decision is rooted in the same theory or concept.

- On those few occasions when a particular decision does not fit into the overarching concept, be sure to explain to her that this decision is an exception or an experiment. Without this explanation she may start to worry that the organization is becoming incoherent.

HOW TO MANAGE A PERSON
STRONG IN INCLUDER

- This person is interested in making everyone feel part of the team. Ask him to work on an orientation program for new employees. He will be excited to think about ways to welcome these new recruits.

- Ask him to lead a task force to recruit minority persons into your organization. He is instinctively sensitive to those who are or have been left out.

- When you have group functions, ask him to make sure that everyone is included. He will work hard to ensure that no individual or group is overlooked.

- In the same vein you can capitalize on this person's Includer theme by focusing it on your customers. Properly positioned, he may prove very effective at breaking the barriers between customer and company.

- Because he probably will not appreciate elite products or services made for a select category of customer, position him to work on products or services that are designed with a broad market in mind. He will enjoy planning ways to open the net wide.

- In certain situations it may be appropriate to ask him to be your organization's link to community social agencies.

HOW TO MANAGE A PERSON STRONG IN INDIVIDUALIZATION

- Ask this person to serve on your selection committee for any number of positions. She will probably be a very good judge of each candidate's strengths and weaknesses.

- Ask her to help improve the organization's productivity by figuring out the right roles for everyone according to their strengths and weaknesses.

- Have her help design pay-for-performance programs where each employee can use his strengths to maximize his pay.

- When you are having difficulty understanding a certain employee's perspective, turn to her for insight. She can show you the world through the employee's eyes.

- When you are having performance problems with individual employees, discuss with her what might be done. Her intuitions about the appropriate action for each individual will be sound.

- When appropriate, ask her to teach an internal training class or mentor a couple of new employees. She may well have a knack for spotting how each person learns a little differently.

- Look at her other dominant themes. If her Developer and Arranger talents are also strong, she may have the potential to be a manager or supervisor. If her strength lies in the themes Command and Woo, she will probably be very effective at turning prospects into customers.

HOW TO MANAGE A PERSON STRONG IN INPUT

- Focus this person's natural inquisitiveness by asking him to research a topic of importance to your organization. He enjoys the knowledge that comes from research.

- Position him in roles with a heavy research component.

- Pay attention to his other strong themes. If he is also strong in Developer, he may excel as a teacher or trainer by peppering his lesson with intriguing facts and stories.

- Keep him posted on the news within your organization. He needs to be in the know. Pass along books, articles, and papers you think he would like to know about and read.

- Encourage him to make use of the Internet. He will use it to find information he thinks he needs. Not all of his fact-finding will be immediately useful, but it will be important for his self-esteem.

- Help him develop a system for storing the information he collects. This system will ensure that he can find it when he and the organization need it.

- When you are in meetings, make a point of asking him for information. Look for opportunities to say something positive about his recall, such as "It's amazing. You always seem to have the facts we need."

HOW TO MANAGE A PERSON STRONG IN INTELLECTION

- Capitalize on the fact that thinking energizes this person. For example, when you have a need to explain why something has to be done, ask her to think it through for you and then provide you with the perfect explanation.

- Don't hesitate to challenge her thinking. She should not be threatened by this. On the contrary she should take it as a sign that you are paying attention to her and be stimulated by it.

- Encourage her to find a few long stretches of time when she can simply muse. For some people pure thinking time is not productive behavior, but for her it is. She will have more clarity and self-confidence as a result.

- When you are faced with books, articles, or proposals that need to be evaluated, ask her to read them and give you a report. She loves to read.

- Have a detailed discussion with her regarding her strengths. She will probably enjoy the introspection and self-discovery.

- Give her the opportunity to present her thinking to other people in the department. The pressure of communicating her thinking to others will force her to refine and clarify her thoughts.

- Be prepared to partner her with someone strong in the Activator theme. This partner will push her to act on her thoughts and ideas.

HOW TO MANAGE A PERSON
STRONG IN LEARNER

- Position this person in roles that require him to stay current in a fast-changing field. He will enjoy the challenge of maintaining his competency.

- Regardless of his role, he will be eager to learn new facts, skills, or knowledge. Explore new ways for him to learn and remain motivated, lest he start hunting for a richer learning environment. For example, if he lacks opportunities to learn on the job, encourage him to take courses that interest him at the local college or association. Remember, he doesn't necessarily need to be promoted; he just needs to be learning. It is the *process* of learning, not the result, that energizes him.

- Help him track his learning progress by identifying milestones or levels that he has reached. Celebrate these milestones.

- In the same vein encourage this person to become the "master of trade" or "resident expert" in his field. Arrange for him to take the relevant classes. Be sure to recognize his learning with the appropriate certificates and plaques.

- Have this person work beside a master who will continuously push him to learn more.

- Ask him to conduct internal discussion groups or presentations. There may be no better way to learn than to teach others.

- Help him secure financial support to continue his education.

HOW TO MANAGE A PERSON STRONG IN MAXIMIZER

- This person is interested in taking something that works and figuring out ways to maximize its performance. She may not be particularly interested in fixing things that are broken.

- Avoid positioning her in roles that demand continual problem solving.

- She will expect you to understand her strengths and to value her for those strengths. She will become frustrated if you spend too much time focusing on her weaknesses.

- Schedule time to discuss her strengths in detail and to strategize how and where these strengths can be used for the organization's advantage. She will enjoy these conversations and offer many practical suggestions for how her strengths can best be used.

- As much as possible, help her develop a career path and a compensation plan that will allow her to keep growing toward excellence in her current role. She will instinctively want to stay on her strengths' path and thus may dislike career structures that force her off this path in order to increase her earning power.

- Ask her to lead a task force to investigate the best practices within your organization. She is naturally inquisitive about excellence.

- Ask her to help design a program for measuring and celebrating the productivity of each employee. She will enjoy thinking about what excellence should look like in each role.

HOW TO MANAGE A PERSON
STRONG IN POSITIVITY

- This person brings drama and energy to the workplace. Find ways to position him as close to your customers as possible. He will make your organization seem more positive and more dynamic.

- Ask him to help plan events in which your organization hosts your best customers, such as new product launches or user groups.

- The Positivity theme does not imply that he is always in a good mood. It does imply that through his humor and attitude he can make people more excited about their work. Remind him of this strength and encourage him to use it.

- He will quickly be sapped of energy by cynics. Don't expect him to enjoy cheering up negative people. He will do better when asked to energize basically positive people who are simply in need of a spark.

- His enthusiasm is contagious. Consider this when placing him on project teams.

- He likes to celebrate. When certain milestones of achievement have been reached, ask him for ideas about how to recognize and celebrate the achievement. He will be more creative than most.

- Pay attention to his other strong themes. If he also possesses strength in the Developer theme, he may prove to be an excellent trainer or teacher, because he brings excitement to the classroom. If Command is one of his strongest themes, he may excel in selling because he is armed with a potent combination of assertiveness and energy.

HOW TO MANAGE A PERSON STRONG IN RELATOR

- Tell this person directly that you care about her. More than likely this language will not sound inappropriate and will be welcomed by her. She organizes her life around her close relationships, so she will want to know where she stands with you.

- She will enjoy developing genuine bonds with the people with whom she works. These relationships take time to build, so don't place her in a role that uproots her frequently from her colleagues and customers.

- Help her know the goals of her colleagues. She is more likely to bond with them when she knows their goals.

- Trust her with confidential information. She is loyal, places a high value on trust, and will not betray yours.

- Ask her to build genuine trusting relationships with the critical people that you want to retain. She can be one of the human ties that bind good people to your organization.

- Pay attention to her other strong themes. If she also shows strong evidence of Focus or Arranger or Self-assurance, she may have the potential to manage others. Employees will always work harder for someone who they know will be there for them and who wants them to succeed. She can easily establish these kinds of relationships.

- Generosity is often a strength of hers. Draw attention to her generosity and show her how it helps her impact and connect with those around her. She will appreciate your noticing, and thus your own relationship will be strengthened.

HOW TO MANAGE A PERSON STRONG IN RESPONSIBILITY

- This person defines himself by his ability to live up to his commitments. It will be intensely frustrating for him to work around people who don't. As far as possible try to avoid putting him in team situations with lackadaisical teammates.

- He defines himself by the quality of his work. He will resist if you force him to rush his work so much that quality suffers. He dislikes sacrificing quality for speed.

- In discussing his work, talk about its quality first.

- Recognize that he is a self-starter and requires little supervision to ensure that assignments are completed.

- Put him in positions requiring unimpeachable ethics. He will not let you down.

- Periodically ask him what new responsibility he would like to assume. It is motivational for him to volunteer, so give him the opportunity.

- Protect him from taking on too much, particularly if he lacks a theme such as Discipline. Help him see that one more burden may result in his dropping the ball, a notion he will loathe.

- He may well impress you with his ability to deliver time and again. You may be so impressed that you decide to promote him to management. *Be careful.* He may much prefer to do a job himself than be responsible for someone else's work, in which case he will find management frustrating. Faced with this situation, help him find other ways to grow.

HOW TO MANAGE A PERSON
STRONG IN RESTORATIVE

- Ask this person for her observations when you want to identify a problem within your organization. Her insights will be particularly acute.

- Position her where she is paid to solve problems for your best customers. She enjoys the challenge of discovering and removing the obstacles.

- When a situation within your organization needs immediate improvement, turn to her for help. She will not panic but instead will respond in a focused, businesslike way.

- When she resolves a problem, make sure to celebrate the achievement. Every wrong situation righted is a success for her, and she will need you to view it as such. Show her that others have come to rely on her ability to dismantle obstacles and move forward.

- Offer your support when she meets a particularly thorny problem. Since she defines herself by her ability to cope, she may well feel personally defeated if the situation remains unresolved. Help her through it.

- Ask her in what ways she would like to improve. Agree that these improvements should serve as goals for the following six months. She will appreciate this kind of attention.

HOW TO MANAGE A PERSON STRONG IN SELF-ASSURANCE

- Give this person a role where he has the leeway to make meaningful decisions. He will neither want nor require close hand-holding.

- Position him in a role where persistence is essential to success. He has the self-confidence to stay the course despite pressure to change direction.

- Put him in a role that demands an aura of certainty and stability. At critical moments this inner authority will calm his colleagues and his customers.

- Support his self-concept that he is an agent of action. Reinforce it with comments such as "It's up to you. You make it happen" or "What is your intuition saying? Let's go with your intuition."

- Help him know that his decisions and actions do produce outcomes. He is at his most effective when he believes he is in control of his world. Highlight practices that work.

- Understand that he may have beliefs about what he can do that might not relate to his actual strengths. Although his self-confidence can often prove useful, if he overclaims or makes some major misjudgments, be sure to point these out immediately. He needs clear feedback to inform his instincts.

- Pay attention to his other strong themes. If he also possesses themes such as Futuristic, Focus, Significance, or Arranger, he may well be a potential leader within your organization.

HOW TO MANAGE A PERSON STRONG IN SIGNIFICANCE

- Be aware of this person's need for independence. Do not over-manage her.

- Acknowledge that she thrives on meaningful recognition for her contributions. Give her room to manuever, but never ignore her. Be sure to feed all compliments through to her.

- Give her the opportunity to stand out, to be known. She enjoys the pressure of being the focal point of attention. Arrange for her to stand out for the right reasons, or she will try to make it happen herself, perhaps inappropriately.

- Position her so that she can associate with credible, productive, professional people. She likes to surround herself with the best.

- Encourage her to praise other top achievers in the group. She enjoys making other people feel successful.

- When she makes claims to excellence—and she will—help her picture the strengths she will have to develop in order to realize these claims. When coaching her, don't ask her to lower her claims; instead, suggest that she keep benchmarks for developing the relevant strengths.

- Because she places such a premium on the perceptions of others, her self-esteem can suffer when others do not give her the recognition she deserves. At these times draw her attention back to her strengths and encourage her to set new goals based on these strengths. These goals will help reenergize her.

HOW TO MANAGE A PERSON STRONG IN STRATEGIC

- Position this person on the leading edge of your organization. His ability to anticipate problems and their solutions will be valuable. For example, ask him to sort through all of the possibilities and find the best way forward for your department. Suggest that he report back on the best strategy.

- Involve him in organizational planning. Ask him, "If this happened, what should we expect?" "If that happened, what should we expect?"

- Always give him ample time to think through a situation before asking for his input. He needs to play out a couple of scenarios in his mind before voicing his opinion.

- Recognize this person's strength in the Strategic theme by sending him to a strategic planning or futurism seminar. The content will sharpen his ideas.

- This person is likely to have a strength for putting his ideas and thoughts into words. To refine his thinking, ask him to present his ideas to his colleagues or to write them for internal distribution.

- When you hear or read of strategies that worked in your field, share them with this person. It will stimulate his thinking.

HOW TO MANAGE A PERSON
STRONG IN WOO

- Try to position this person in a role where she has a chance to meet new people every day. Strangers energize her.

- Place her at your organization's initial point of contact with the outside world. She can put strangers at ease and help them feel comfortable with your organization.

- Help her refine her system for remembering the names of the people she meets. Set a goal for her to learn the names and a few personal details about as many customers as possible. She can help your organization make many connections in the market-place.

- Unless she is also strong in themes such as Empathy and Relator, do not expect her to enjoy a role where she is asked to build close relationships with your customers. Instead, she may well prefer to meet and greet, win over, and move on to the next.

- Her strength in Woo will win you over and cause you to like her. When considering her for new roles and responsibilities, make sure that you look past your liking of her to her genuine strengths. Don't let her Woo theme dazzle you.

- If possible, ask her to be the builder of goodwill for your organization within the community. Have her represent your organization at community clubs and meetings.

CHAPTER 7

Building a Strengths-based Organization

- **THE FULL STORY**
- **THE PRACTICAL GUIDE**

The Full Story

"Who is leading the strengths revolution at work?"

In the introduction to this book we noted that in response to the question "At work do you have the opportunity to do what you do best every day?" only 20 percent of employees could answer "strongly agree." And we used this discovery to kick-start the strengths revolution at work. Now we have a confession to make. The data showing that 20 percent of employees "strongly agree" are accurate but incomplete. To give you the full story we need to mine the database more deeply.

Some organizations have already begun the strengths revolution. The 75th percentile in our database is 33 percent, which means that in these organizations a third of employees strongly agree that they are using their strengths every day. The 90th percentile is at a whopping 45 percent of employees saying "strongly agree." And when you examine the database still closer, you discover even more impressive examples of strengths-based workplaces. Ralph Gonzalez, the Best Buy manager we mentioned in the previous chapter who leads one hundred employees on the retail front lines, has developed the kind of work environment where 50 percent of them strongly agree. In Boca Raton, Florida, another Best Buy store manager, Mary Garey, has somehow created the kind of workplace in which 70 percent of her employees feel that they are perfectly cast in their roles. This means that in Mary's store seventy of her one hundred employees, most of whom are engaged in customer service, loading/unloading, or shelf-stocking roles, strongly agree that at work they have an opportunity to do what they do best every day.

Mary and Ralph are exceptional, but in virtually every organization where we have asked this question, we have found similar exceptions. In fact, perhaps the most compelling discovery gleaned from our research is the huge range of responses that this question elicits. No matter how large the organization, no matter what its business or its location, we invariably find some managers whose work groups are in the top 5 percent and some managers whose work groups lie in the bottom 5 percent. Even if all the employees are involved in the same kind of work, this massive range nonetheless appears.

The standard set by managers like Ralph and Mary frames the questions that this chapter will attempt to answer: How can you narrow the range? How can you create an entire organization that employs the strengths of every person as efficiently as your best managers do? Restated more numerically, how can you create an entire organization where at least 45 percent of your employees (the 90th percentile) strongly agree that they are using their strengths every day?

The more you ponder the question "At work, do I have an opportunity to do what I do best every day?" the more complex it becomes. There are many reasons that a particular employee in a particular role might say no. He might genuinely feel that he lacks the talent to do the job. Or perhaps he possesses the talent, but the organization has overlegislated the role so that he has no chance to express his talents. Perhaps he feels he has the talents and room to use them but not the necessary skills or knowledge. Perhaps objectively he is perfectly cast, but subjectively he feels he has much more to offer. Perhaps he is right, or perhaps he is deluding himself as to where his true strengths lie. Perhaps he was perfectly cast in his previous role but was promoted into the wrong role because the organization couldn't think of any other way to reward him. Perhaps the organization sends signals that it is a "pass-through" role, and thus no self-respecting employee will ever say he is well cast in it even if he knows he is.

At first glance this complexity can be overwhelming. To address all these possibilities and thus ensure that your employees say "strongly agree" to the question, you would have to attend to many different aspects of each employee's working life. To address his fear that he lacks the talent for the role, you would have to be careful to select people who seem to possess talents similar to your best incumbents in the role. To avoid the overlegislation problem, you would have to hold him accountable for his performance but not define, step by step, how he should achieve the desired performance. To overcome his fear that he lacks the necessary skills and knowledge, you would have to construct coaching programs that help him develop his talents into genuine strengths. To address the "delusion" issue you would have to devise a way to have every manager help each employee discover and appreciate his true strengths. To avoid the "overpromotion" problem you would have to provide him with alternative ways to grow in money and title other than simply climbing the corporate ladder. And, finally, to deal with his perception that he is in a "pass-through" role, you would have to send the message that no role is by definition a pass-through role. Any role performed at excellence is genuinely respected within the organization.

Listed back to back like this, the challenges associated with building an entire organization around the strengths of each employee appear almost incoherent, "try a bit of this, do a bit of that." But dwell on them for a moment, and you may soon realize that all these challenges cohere around two core assumptions about people:

1. Each person's talents are enduring and unique.

2. Each person's greatest room for growth is in the areas of the person's greatest strength.

As you can see, we have come full circle. We presented these assumptions earlier as insights into human nature that all great managers seem to share. What we are saying now is that as long as everything you do is founded on these two core assumptions, you will successfully address the many challenges contained in the question "At work, do I have the opportunity to do what I do best every day?" You will build an entire organization around the strengths of each employee. Why? Let's play out these two assumptions and see where they lead:

- Since each person's talents are enduring, *you should spend a great deal of time and money selecting people properly in the first place.* This will help mitigate the "I don't think I have the right talent for the role" problem.

- Since each person's talents are unique, *you should focus performance by legislating outcomes* rather than forcing each person into a stylistic mold. This means a strong emphasis on careful measurement of the right outcomes, and less on policies, procedures, and competencies. This will address the "in my role I don't have any room to express my talents" problem.

- Since the greatest room for each person's growth is in the areas of his greatest strength, *you should focus your training time and money on educating him about his strengths and figuring out ways to build on these strengths* rather than on remedially trying to plug his "skill gaps." You will find that this one shift in emphasis will pay huge dividends. In one fell swoop you will sidestep three potential pitfalls to building a strengths-based organization: the "I don't have the skills and knowledge I need" problem, the "I don't know what I'm best at" problem, and the "my manager doesn't know what I'm best at" problem.

- Lastly, since the greatest room for each person's growth lies in his areas of greatest strength, *you should devise ways to help each person grow his career without necessarily promoting him up the corporate ladder and out of his areas of strength.* In this organization "promotion" will mean finding ways to give prestige, respect, and financial reward to anyone who has achieved world-class performance in any role, no matter where that role is in the hierarchy. By doing so you will overcome the remaining two obstacles to building a strengths-based organization: the "even though I'm now in the wrong role, it was the only way to grow my career" problem and the "I'm in a pass-through role that no one respects" problem.

These four steps represent a systematic process for maximizing the value locked up in your human capital. In the pages that follow we flesh out this process. We offer you a practical guide for how to use those two core assumptions to change the way you select, measure, develop, and channel the careers of your people. Needless to say the individual manager will always be a critical catalyst in transforming each employee's talents into bona fide strengths; consequently, much of the responsibility will lie with the manager to select for talent, set clear expectations, focus on strengths, and develop each employee's career. Taking the ideas found in *First, Break All the Rules* a step further, however, we have aimed this practical guide at the challenges facing larger organizations as they strive to capitalize on the strengths of every employee.

The Practical Guide

"How can you build a strengths-based organization?"

- The Strengths-based Selection System
- The Strengths-based Performance Management System
- The Strengths-based Career Development System

THE STRENGTHS-BASED SELECTION SYSTEM

The perfect selection system is an integrated affair involving a myriad of activities—recruiting, interviewing, measuring, educating, tracking, and so on—which in a large organization must occur all the time. For the sake of clarity, however, we will present this system as a simple sequence of five steps. If you were to start from scratch, this is the order you would follow.

First, you need to *build your selection system around an instrument for measuring talent*. A number of such instruments exist, but whichever one you choose must meet two rigorous standards: It must be psychometrically sound, which means that it must measure what it purports to measure, and it must rely on objective scoring, which means that if two, three, or even one hundred people analyzed a particular person's responses, they would all arrive at the same results. This doesn't imply that all these analysts would reach the same conclusions about the best role for or the best way to manage this particular person, but it does imply that they should all be using exactly the same data to reach their unique conclusions.

If you don't establish this objective instrument as your foundation—if, say, you simply rely on training managers to be better interviewers or on the ratings of professional observers at an assessment center or on any other method with inherent "interrater reliability" problems (this means different raters giving the same candidate different ratings on his strengths and weaknesses)—your whole selection system will be handicapped from the outset. Lacking data that are 100 percent reliable, you will be unable to investigate the links between measured talent and subsequent performance. (For various arcane mathematical reasons, data derived from a system plagued with interrater reliability problems are virtually unusable.) For example, you will never be able to discover which talents drive higher customer satisfaction scores or better safety records or lower employee turnover or faster recovery of hospital patients. In all your analyses the talent factor will be absent, leaving you functionally blind as to the effect of each employee's talents on the important outcomes of your business. Intuitively you will know that each employee's talents affect your business in some way, but you'll never know where or how much.

We are not suggesting, of course, that you shouldn't train managers to be better interviewers or that assessment centers are a complete waste of time and money, but we are saying that these techniques are inappropriate foundations for the perfect selection system. To use a well-worn analogy: Manager interviews, assessment centers, and the like are analog techniques cursed with all the accompanying inefficiencies (lack of precision, lack of comparability, lack of consistency). By contrast, an objective talent measurement instrument is a digital technique. Used properly it serves as the consistent operating system on which all your other "software"—your business analyses, your recruiting strategies, your manpower planning—can run.

The second step in building your selection system is to *calibrate your instrument by studying your best performers in each key role.* This can begin with a simple focus group where you ask a series of open-ended questions to get a feel for the role, but by far the most rigorous approach is to conduct a full concurrent validity study. Intimidating though it sounds, executing a concurrent validity study is actually rather straightforward: you administer the talent instrument to every employee in the role in question, collect performance scores on these employees, and use these scores to identify a study group of fifty or more employees (the most effective in the role) and a contrast group of a similar number (the least effective). If your organization lacks objective performance scores, you will have to use the folk definition of your most effective, namely, "Who are the ones you would want to hire more of?" Then you calibrate your instrument by identifying the responses and talents shared by the study group and absent in the contrast group. This last step requires someone with statistical expertise, but the net result is an instrument calibrated for the role and an understanding of some of the dominant talents necessary for excellence in the role.

The third step is to *teach the talent language throughout the organization.* This is important for a number of reasons, not the least of which is that you want your managers to make the final hiring decision, and a full understanding of talent language will help them make better decisions. Many organizations centralize most recruiting activities, as they should. Human beings are infuriatingly complicated, and consequently it makes sense to establish a department, usually the human resources department, to cultivate expertise in understanding this complexity. Just as you expect your IT department to influence the high-tech resources your managers use, so you should expect your HR department to influence the human resources they use. However, this comparison isn't entirely appropriate. Employees aren't computers. They don't come with a users' manual or on/off switches. To reach their full capacity and potential, they require a manager whom they trust, who expects the best from them, and who takes the time to learn their idiosyncracies. In short, they require a relationship. And this relationship starts or stalls at the point of hire.

So teach your managers the talent language. Supply them with qualified candidates using your calibrated instrument. Then show them each candidate's dominant talents and encourage them to use these talents to make as informed a decision as possible. Yes, they will occasionally make hiring mistakes, but these mistakes are less important in the larger scheme. To build a strengths-based organization demands that your managers become personally invested in their employees' success, and they are unlikely to get invested if you are constantly forcing employees on them from headquarters.

Another reason to teach the language of talents throughout the organization is that you can then use this language in recruiting. If you peruse the employment opportunities section of your local newspaper, the first thing you will notice is the irrelevance of talent. Most employment advertisements loudly assert the need for certain skills, knowledge, and years of experience but remain mute on talent. It is ironic that they itemize the qualities they can change in a person while ignoring the ones they can't.

A strengths-based organization shouldn't make this mistake. Having identified the dominant talents needed for the role, you should craft employment advertisements that challenge the applicant to claim these talents. For example, let's say that you discovered from your concurrent validity study that the dominant talents for a computer programmer were Analytical (an ordered, numbers-oriented mind), Discipline (a need for structure), Arranger (an ability to coordinate the demands of a fluid environment), and Learner (a love of the process of acquiring competence in something). Your employment advertisement might then use the following questions as the centerpiece:

- Do you take a logical and systematic approach to problem solving? (Analytical)

- Are you a perfectionist who strives for timely completion of your projects? (Discipline)

- Can you prioritize the urgency of multiple requests and then take charge to meet these deadlines? (Arranger)

- Do you want to learn how to use SQL, Java, and Perl, and build world-class database-driven Web sites? (Learner)

If you can say yes to these questions, then please call . . .

You may still require certain skills and experience levels, but with those four questions in the center of the layout in bold type, you will be catching the eye and challenging the reader to claim these qualities. Naturally, some readers who don't possess them will still apply, but many won't, so you will end up with fewer applicants of a higher quality, the perfect measure of an effective employment advertisement.

The fourth step in the construction of your selection system is to *build a theme profile of your entire company,* a theme inventory, if you will. This theme inventory serves two distinct functions. First, it provides you with a snapshot of the character of your company. On one level this has nice-to-know value. Perhaps yours is a competitive culture with no service orientation (strong in Competition, weak in Belief). Or perhaps yours is a service-oriented culture that lacks openness to new ways of doing things (strong in Belief, weak in Ideation and Strategic).

But on another level this all-company snapshot has a distinctly practical value in that it will allow you to align your human resources strategy with your business strategy. For example, let's say that your organization, a bank, has realized that the tellers in your branches must become more sales-oriented if you are to execute your cross-selling business strategy. In the past you might have tried to retrain your branch tellers to become salespeople, with the usual disastrous results: Many tellers are proud of their client responsiveness but view selling as one step up from the devil.

Now you can take a more sophisticated approach. You can look at your entire population of tellers and identify those who possess talents that suggest a more sales-oriented mentality, talents such as Activator, Command, and Woo. You can then invest heavily in training these tellers in the skills and knowledge required to cross-sell, and redesign your branch teams so that these retrained tellers lead the sales initiatives with clients, leaving the other tellers to do what they do best—provide excellent client service.

The preceding example presupposes that you have to fight the war with the army you have. This is sometimes the case, but often an organization has the leeway to use its all-company theme inventory to recruit a different army. For example, let's suppose that your theme inventory reveals that your entire cadre of front-line managers is strong in such talents as Achiever, Consistency, and Focus. (Incidentally, this often happens. A person strong in these three talents is self-motivated, sets clear expectations, and doesn't trample those around him. These are exactly the sort of qualities that get a person promoted into management.) However, let's also suppose that this cadre of managers is weak in such talents as Individualization, Maximizer, and Relator. Given the enduring nature of talent, no amount of retraining will help this current cadre of managers excel at building relationships with their employees, getting to know their strengths, and setting them up for success. Stuck with this army, your organization will always struggle to keep and develop talented employees.

This discovery needn't depress you. You can now avoid wasting millions retraining these managers and invest in selecting a new cadre that does possess these talents. Here we are not suggesting that you replace your entire existing cadre with the new; this is neither possible nor desirable. Rather, we are saying that as you move each new person into management, you should examine his or her profile closely to see whether or not that person possesses strength in the talents where the majority are weak. Gradually but deliberately you will change the character of your company, one character at a time.

The other function this theme inventory serves is to help channel each employee's career for a long while after he is brought on board. As you know, an organization is a fluid community, with employees moving in and out of different roles as they and the organization grow. For an organization to remain vital and strong it should take each employee's talents into account when deciding the moves that are appropriate for each employee. This rarely happens. Most organizations keep track of their employees' skills, knowledge, and work experience but ignore their talents. Even if some theme information is gathered at the point of hire, it is lost soon after, never to be referred to again.

Your selection system must avoid this fundamental flaw. Use a theme inventory to capture and keep each employee's talent profile. Set up a mechanism (either intranet, Internet, or physical) so that the appropriate people can refer to an employee's theme profile when considering him for internal career moves. Far from limiting this person's career choices, his theme profile should encourage you to consider him for dramatic career moves even if he doesn't possess the necessary skills, knowledge, or work experience. As mentioned in Chapter 5, in any career move the person will bring his talents with him. You can always teach him the rest.

The last step in building a strengths-based selection system is to *study the links between measured talent and subsequent performance.* Many human resources departments have an inferiority complex. With the best of intentions they do everything they can to highlight the importance of people, but when sitting around the boardroom table, they suspect that they don't get the same respect as finance, marketing, or operations. In many instances they are right, but, unfortunately, in many instances they don't deserve to. Why? Because they don't have any data. Most chief executives know that the quality of their people somehow affects their business results, but they rightly expect much more detailed explanations. Here are just a few examples of the kinds of questions for which an effective chief executive should expect answers:

- How good are our recruiting efforts? From where do we find the most talented candidates—universities, competitors, the armed forces, the local paper, the Internet? How do we know one way or another?

- Which kind of people are shooting stars, extremely productive out of the chute but prone to fade and leave the organization? How do we know?

- Are we raising the talent level of our managers with each person promoted? How do we know?

- What kind of people have the talent to be future leaders? How many of them do we have? Are we deliberately hiring more like them? How do we know?

- Are we investing our training budget in our most talented people? How do we know?

- What kinds of people get good ratings from our managers but low ratings from our customers? How do we know?

Lacking any kind of objectively measured talent data, even the most experienced human resources director will be stumped for answers. But armed with data he can describe in detail the links between measured talent and subsequent performance. As an example, let's take the last of these questions: What kinds of people get good ratings from our managers but low ratings from our customers?

Working with a large telecommunications company, Gallup was given access to the manager evaluations of over five thousand employees who interfaced with customers, the employees' individual theme profiles, and their performance ratings from customers. (For each employee fifteen customers per month were contacted and asked to rate the quality of service received. The study lasted ten months, for a total of 150 customer ratings for each employee.) We threw all these data into the hopper and tried to tease apart the links.

The first discovery was this: The employees who were strong in the themes Responsibility and Harmony earned the highest evaluations from their managers, which, if you think about it, makes sense. If an employee consistently shows up on time and doesn't make a fuss, he is likely to endear himself to his boss. Primed with this discovery the human resources director might be tempted to say to her chief executive, "If we want to improve our manager evaluation scores, we should hire more people with Responsibility and Harmony." Unfortunately, if this advice were offered and followed, it would take the company in the wrong direction because our second discovery was that there was no link between the manager evaluations and the customer ratings. Stated numerically, the statistical correlation between these two sets of data was zero. Whatever behaviors the managers were evaluating were irrelevant to the customers. The managers might as well have been rating the employees' shoe size for all the customers cared.

It was the third and final discovery that led to the correct course of action. We found that the themes that correlated to each employee's customer ratings were not Responsibility and Harmony but Achiever, Positivity, Learner, Command, and Restorative. These employees were self-motivated, energetic and upbeat, excited to learn, and assertive enough to take control of each customer's predicament and solve the problem (and also assertive enough to challenge their manager if they disagreed with him, which probably accounted for their lower manager evaluation scores). Guided by this discovery the company could do two things: It could refocus its recruiting and selection initiatives on these five critical themes, and it could jettison its complicated manager evaluation process and replace it with the more objective performance measure: customer satisfaction scores.

The best human resources departments must learn the language of business. They must be able to explain mathematically the subtle but significant effects of human nature on business results. Only then will they prove themselves as valuable as the other departments and garner the respect they truly deserve.

THE STRENGTHS-BASED PERFORMANCE MANAGEMENT SYSTEM

Once you have discovered each person's strongest talents, the obvious goal is to focus and develop these talents into measurable performance. All organizations would most likely agree with this. More surprising, most organizations would also agree on the three key areas of performance worth focusing on.

1. The person's impact on the business, such as number of sales made for a salesperson, number of errors per million for a manufacturing team, shrinkage percentage for a store manager, or growth in profits for a restaurant manager.

2. The person's impact on the customer, either internal or external. Organizations have different ways of investigating this—mystery shopper programs, call-out surveys, in-room surveys, the monitoring of customer calls, and so on—but the focus is the same: the quality of service received by the customer.

3. And last, the person's impact on the employees around him. Again, organizations use different methods to address this— 360-degree surveys measuring each employee on various behaviors, employee surveys, qualitative manager evaluations—but whatever the system of choice, the point is to hold each person accountable for his influence on the culture of the organization.

Agreement vanishes, however, when it comes to what actions the organization should take to improve a person's performance in these areas. Conceptually speaking, the world of what is often called "performance management" can be split into two distinct camps. Both camps share a belief in the fundamental importance and potential of their employees, but only one of them will create the kind of environment where that potential is realized. Only one of them will lead to a workplace built on the strengths of each employee. And, unfortunately, at present this strengths-based camp is very much in the minority.

The larger, establishment camp is comprised of those organizations that legislate the *process* of performance. If performance is a journey from the individual to the results, these organizations choose to focus on the steps of this journey. They apply their creativity to the challenge of defining the journey in detail, and having defined it, they try to teach each employee to walk the same path.

These step-by-step organizations share many characteristics, such as overscripting of employees and over-reliance on process reengineering, but perhaps their clearest identifying mark is their current fascination with managerial competencies. To improve each manager's impact on the culture these organizations identify a list of desired behaviors or "competencies" (for example, "uses humor appropriately," "accepts change," or "thinks strategically") and then spend a great deal of time and money teaching each manager to acquire these competencies. Because style training is the focus and the measurement of true performance is an afterthought in this kind of organization, the most pressing question becomes "Since we are investing so much in these competencies, how can we measure if people are actually getting better at them?"

For the second camp, the strengths-based camp, this question is irrelevant. This type of organization focuses not on the steps of the journey but on the end of the journey—namely, the right way to measure each person's results in the three key areas. The coaching efforts of these organizations are then designed to help people find their own paths to the prescribed end. These organizations do not struggle to measure the effectiveness of this coaching. They *start* by defining the right outcome measures and then construct the coaching to drive these measures. If the measures move up, the training is effective. If they don't, then it isn't.

The step-by-step camp will still measure some performance outcomes (particularly in the area of business results), and, likewise, the strengths-based camp will define and teach some processes (every clothing designer must know how to cut cloth; every loan officer must learn how to qualify the bank's customers). Nonetheless, the distinction between the two camps is real. Step-by-step organizations are designed to battle the inherent individuality of each employee. Strengths-based organizations are designed to capitalize on it.

So what can your organization do to join the ranks of the strengths-based camp? We suggest four steps.

The first step is to *figure out the right way to measure the desired performance,* the end of the journey, if you will. In the area of business results this is fairly straightforward. Using a simple question such as "What do the employees in this role get paid to do?" you can focus your thinking and arrive at the right metrics for the role. Even here, however, there is some room for creativity. The hundreds of technical support specialists at Cox Communications' customer care center just outside San Diego, California, are measured not only on obvious metrics such as talk time (average length of call) and sign-on time (average percentage of the working day each one is actually on the phone with customers) but also on a rather more exotic metric, "truck rolls." A truck roll occurs when the support specialist is unable to solve the customer's problem over the phone and has to dispatch a repair truck to the customer's home. Since this often proves inconvenient for the customer, support specialists are encouraged to roll as few trucks as possible.

As you work to define these business results metrics for every key role, don't be discouraged by employees who claim "You can't measure my role. It's too fluid and dynamic and subjective." They may be right. Their role might be all these things, but in today's fast-changing business world, the same can be said for every role. To be sure, some roles are more affected by changes than others, but the fact is that all roles, no matter how dynamic, are designed to produce certain outcomes. You should be able to count, rate, or rank some, if not most, of these outcomes. With enough insight and creativity you'll find that there is indeed a truck roll for every role.

Measuring each employee's impact on the customer is a little more difficult. The customers of Cox Communications' support specialists obviously expect kinds of service that are very different from the kinds that customers of tellers in a bank expect. Likewise, a department's external customers will have demands that are very different from the same department's internal customers. Faced with this variety, many organizations design role-specific questionnaires in order to analyze each step in the employee-customer interaction. Unfortunately, these lengthy questionnaires overcomplicate matters. They can occasionally prove useful as diagnostic tools—"Exactly what is going on when our employees and customers interact?"—

but because of their unwieldy complexity, they are virtually useless as performance measures.

A more effective approach is to design a simple way to measure the emotional outcomes you want to create in your customers, whether internal or external. You can then hold each employee accountable for creating these emotions, using whatever strengths each happens to possess. Culled from Gallup's extensive research into customer loyalty, we offer these three questions as a simple and accurate metric for measuring the employee's impact on the customer, both external and internal:

1. Overall, how well did the service you received meet your expectations? Was it much better than expected . . . much worse than expected?

2. How likely are you to recommend this product/service to others? Are you very likely . . . very unlikely?

3. How likely are you to want to continue using this product/service? Are you very likely . . . very unlikely?

With current technology it is a relatively straightforward task to link a particular employee to a particular customer. By asking these three questions directly of your customers (either internal or external) you can avoid the potential bias or, as we saw earlier, the possible irrelevance of manager evaluations and instead glean an accurate reading of each employee's actual impact on the customer.

Measuring each employee's impact on his fellow employees can prove equally challenging. The relationship between each manager and his employees, and between each employee and his peers, is so multifaceted that you can hardly blame the organizations that attempt to legislate this relationship with predetermined competencies. To reiterate what we said before, though, we suggest that a more effective approach is to measure the *outcomes* of a productive culture and then hold each manager accountable for creating these outcomes, using the style that fits her best. The following twelve questions define the outcomes of a productive culture. We recommend asking each manager's employees these twelve questions, using a 5-point scale (5 for "strongly agree," 1 for "strongly disagree).

1. Do I know what is expected of me at work?

2. Do I have the materials and equipment I need to do my work properly?

3. At work do I have the opportunity to do what I do best every day?

4. In the last seven days have I received recognition or praise for good work?

5. Does my supervisor or someone at work seem to care about me as a person?

6. Is there someone at work who encourages my development?

7. At work do my opinions seem to count?

8. Does the mission of my company make me feel like my work is important?

9. Are my coworkers committed to doing quality work?

10. Do I have a best friend at work?

11. In the last six months have I talked with someone about my progress?

12. This last year have I had opportunities at work to learn and grow?

If you have read *First, Break All the Rules,* you will know that these questions were selected from a list of hundreds precisely because, when worded in exactly this fashion (complete with qualifiers such as "every day," and "in the last seven days," and "best friend"), they predicted employee turnover, productivity, profitability, and customer loyalty. Asked twice a year, they provide the most robust and the most relevant measure of a manager's impact on his employees.

And yet they don't force every manager to manage in the same way. Taking the first question, "Do I know what is expected of me at work?" as an example, an organization shouldn't care that one manager sets expectations by having detailed, one-on-one conversations with each employee while another manager prefers using weekly team meetings to provide the focus, just as long as, at the end of six months, the employees know what is expected of them. Again, the desired end is legislated, not the journey.

And what about the impact of each employee on his peers? The twelve questions presented above don't cover this because they are designed to address manager-employee relations, not employee-employee relations. So, instead, try using these four questions, also culled from our research into highly productive workplaces:

Does this person perform his/her work

1. in a timely manner?

2. in an accurate fashion?

3. in a positive, helpful manner?

4. in a way that makes you feel your opinions count?

Using your organization's intranet, you can field this short survey twice a year by asking every employee to identify the individuals with whom they have had significant contact in the last six months, and you can capture their ratings of these people anonymously on a scale of 1 to 5.

Armed with these three outcome measures—business results, impact on the customer, and impact on the culture—you can now take the remaining three steps toward building a strengths-based performance management system.

The second step is to *build a performance scorecard for every employee.* Much has been made lately of the need for large organizations to use a balanced scorecard to measure their overall performance. In their book *The Balanced Scorecard,* Robert Kaplan and David Norton suggest that you can only assess the true strength of an organization by measuring many different aspects of the organization's performance. Classical performance metrics such as profit growth and revenue growth are trailing measures—"gross approximations of the recent past," as one economist described them—and therefore they reveal little about the organization's future. If you want to predict how healthy the organization will be down the road, you need to add leading indicators to this scorecard, such as whether the organization has a growing number of loyal customers, how engaged its employees are, and whether it is strengthening its talent pool with every hire.

This thinking is so sound that it should be applied to every employee. Every employee should be given a balanced scorecard that provides an objective picture of his or her total performance. This scorecard's dials should reflect performance data from each of the three performance areas—business results, impact on the customer, and impact on the culture. It should be simple to read and have, ideally, one summary number for each of the three performance areas and one comparison number (either the 50th percentile for each dial or, if you like to stretch your people with an image of best practices, the 75th percentile). And it should be updated twice a year, at a minimum.

This scorecard will serve two purposes. First, it will communicate to each employee what success is in his role. This seems obvious, but you would be surprised at how many employees don't know how their success is measured. In fact, in our database of 1.7 million employees, fully 67 percent of them cannot strongly agree with the statement "I know what is expected of me at work." The concern here is not only that because they don't know what is expected of them, they won't know how to focus and prioritize their time. The more significant implication is that since they don't know how their success will be measured, they will never have a chance to feel successful in the organization.

Second, this scorecard will reinforce the values of the organization for every employee. It is one thing to cajole managers to treat their employees respectfully. It is another to hold them accountable twice a year for their employees' response to those twelve questions. The same applies to each employee's impact on the customer and on his peers. Measurement shines a revealing, quantitative spotlight on qualitative values.

The third step is to *ensure that every manager has a strengths discussion with every employee.* Of all the steps this is the one missed most often. So many organizations ignore each employee's unique talents and assume that employees in the same role require the same kind of management. To use an analogy, these organizations play checkers with their employees. They assume that all employees in the same role have similar moves and therefore they all respond to the same kind of training, learn in the same fashion, and require the same level of supervision, with the novices needing slightly more and the experienced slightly less.

By contrast, strengths-based organizations play chess with their people. They understand that each piece moves differently, and if they don't know which piece is which, they might end up treating a rook like a knight and a knight like a rook, which will frustrate the rook and the knight, causing the player to lose the game. So at the outset they place a premium on taking the time to learn each piece's strongest moves. Some of these strength moves are a function of the piece's skills, knowledge, and experience, but many are caused by a particular talent or combination of talents.

When each employee is hired or when a new manager-employee relationship begins, create the expectation that a strengths discussion must take place. The form of this discussion will vary depending on the style of the manager, but it should always cover the following areas:

- What are the employee's strongest themes?

- How do these relate to performance on the job? What style do they produce?

- What skills can the employee learn or what experiences can he have to build these talents into genuine strengths?

- How does the employee like to be managed? (What is the best praise he ever received? Is he likely to tell his manager how he is feeling, or will the manager always have to ask? Is he a very independent person, or does he like to have regular check-ins with his manager? And so on. If your organization uses the StrengthsFinder Profile, the manager action items will prove useful here.)

These strengths discussions can touch on other areas, such as the employee's personal situation or his professional goals, but these four areas should serve as the main focus.

Aside from some practical insights for the manager, the most significant benefit from these discussions will be the employee's awareness of the organization's interest in his strengths. If you want to keep a talented employee, show him not just that you care about him, not just that you will help him grow, but, more important, that you *know* him, that in the truest sense of the word you recognize him (or, at the very least, that you are trying to). In today's increasingly anonymous and transient working world, your organization's inquisitiveness about the strengths of its employees will set your organization apart.

This recognition doesn't mean that you will let him get away with more. On the contrary, it means that you will stretch him more and challenge him more. You want more from him precisely because you know where his greatest potential for excellence lies. And now he knows you know. *His awareness of your awareness of his strengths*—this is the best way to kick-start his journey toward optimum performance.

So now you have your metrics measuring the end of his journey, his performance. You have your balanced scorecard to track his journey. And at the outset you have the beginnings of a relationship founded on his awareness that you are inquisitive about his strengths. To complete your performance management system you need a mechanism to tie these pieces together. You need a way to channel his strengths along his path of least resistance to performance.

The worthy efforts of many human resources and training departments aside, the employee's manager is by far the most influential partner on his journey; therefore, the best mechanism for channeling the employee's path toward performance must by definition be *regular, predictable, and productive meetings with his immediate manager.* If, along with all the other steps we described, you can ensure that your managers meet with each of their employees for at least one hour per quarter to discuss performance, you will almost certainly double the number of employees who strongly agree that they use their strengths every day.

This seems almost too simple, and in some senses it is. There are many actions you can take to add sophistication to these meetings. For example, you can study the methods of your best performers in each key role, capture these different methods in a formal coaching guide, and then encourage your managers to refer to them if they are struggling to offer advice to an employee. Or, as we described in *First, Break All the Rules,* you can train your managers to focus each meeting on three basic questions:

- What will the employee's main focus be for the next three months?

- What new discoveries (or items of learning) is he planning?

- What new partnerships (or relationships) is he hoping to build?

Techniques such as these can certainly be helpful, but the bottom line is that even without these fine-tunings, regular, predictable meetings with a manager are extraordinarily powerful. There are many reasons why. They create a constant tension to achieve—the employee to keep reaching short-term goals, and the manager to keep adding value. They bring the manager closer to the action, which makes it easier to empathize with the employee and easier to spot early clues to a sea change in the marketplace. They provide the manager with the detail needed to see the subtle differences between one employee and another. They are the forum in which generic training is tailored to fit the particular needs of each employee. And, of course, they serve to build the relationship between the two of them.

In fact, there is so much dynamism and so much individuality in today's working world that it is virtually impossible to build a strengths-based organization without these meetings. Everything else you do from the center—conduct concurrent validity studies, build theme profiles, design measurement systems—will be diminished if your managers are not meeting regularly and predictably with each of their people. These meetings are a core regimen of strong organizations.

THE STRENGTHS-BASED CAREER DEVELOPMENT

Your last hurdle to building a strengths-based organization is this: You cannot capitalize on people's strengths if you keep promoting them into roles that don't fit their strengths.

We've known about the dangers of overpromotion for at least the last thirty years (the book *The Peter Principle,* which described how most people are promoted to their level of incompetence, was published in the late 1960s), so why do we keep doing it? Because we want to give people the chance to grow? Because we don't want people to stagnate in their role? Because we want to offer them a career? Because we want to reward them for work well done? No doubt we are influenced by all these sensible intentions. Yet none of them necessarily entails promoting the person. People can learn, grow their careers, and receive praise for good work without getting promoted. And so the question remains: When it comes to development, career growth, or praise, why do we so often resort to moving the person up the ladder? Unless we can get to the heart of this, thirty years from now the Peter Principle will be as deeply ingrained in organizations as it is today, millions of employees will feel miscast, and organizations everywhere will be the weaker for it.

We offer you this explanation: Most organizations keep

promoting people because of a dangerous combination of one great insight and one great error. The one great insight is the intuitive understanding that a craving for prestige is perhaps the most powerful of all human motivations. As Frank Fukuyama described in his book *The End of History and the Last Man,* throughout the centuries many of our wisest thinkers have identified the "need to be recognized as a worthy and significant person" as the essence of being human: "Plato spoke of *thymos,* or 'spiritedness,' Machiavelli of man's desire for glory, Hobbes of his pride or vainglory, Rousseau of his *amour-propre,* Alexander Hamilton of the love of fame and James Madison of ambition, Hegel of recognition, and Nietzsche of man as 'the beast with red cheeks.' " None of these thinkers meant to imply that we are all egotists. They were simply saying that deep in our pysche each of us needs to be viewed as an individual worthy of respect and that this need is so powerful we will risk life and limb in order to fulfill it.

Most of us don't need Hegel, Nietzsche, or Plato to convince us of this. Most of us sense it intuitively. In all our interactions, from our playground squabbles to humanity's noblest battles against oppression, we recognize the moral authority of the voice that says, "Treat me with the respect I deserve as a human being." This insight explains why we know instinctively that prejudice is wrong, that the natural human condition is liberty, and that the best way to honor someone is to give her more prestige.

And we are right to think that way. If you want to imagine what would befall an organization that forgot that insight and thereby failed to satisfy each person's need for prestige, look at what befell Communism. Communism's demise was inevitable (eventually) because it offered respect to the community but never the individual, and so it drained itself of vitality and spirit, one person at a time. The same can be said of those recent experiments to remove hierarchy from organizations and create flat, self-managed teams where no one is in charge and everyone carries the title "Associate." Wonderful in theory, they fail in practice precisely because they frustrate each individual's craving for prestige.

If our one great insight is that all human beings crave prestige and that this craving must be channeled, not ignored or repressed, what is our one great error? Our great error is thinking that all human beings crave the same kind of prestige—the prestige that comes with power. Up until about twenty years ago this wouldn't have been an error. In highly authoritarian societies where each person's freedom of decision, of judgment, and of discretion is at the whim of the person above, the only prestige worth having is the prestige that comes with power over others. And up until twenty years ago most organizations with centralized command and control cultures were highly authoritarian societies. No wonder everyone scrambled up the ladder as fast as they could. It was the only way to avoid being controlled. It was the only way to get respect.

Today, however, many organizations are moving away from command and control and toward more empowered cultures. They have to. In our knowledge economy where specialized expertise and individualized customer relationships are prized, the chances are that the employees know more about their particular field or customers than their manager does, and thus the threat that he has power over their decisions, judgment, and discretion loses much of its force. In these kinds of organizations, who warrants more prestige, the genius programmer or her boss? The superstar salesperson or his sales manager? The inspirational store manager or her district supervisor?

The answer is that in a knowledge economy (and a tight labor market, to boot) anyone who is excelling in his or her role, whether individual contributor, supervisor, manager, or leader, deserves prestige. *Many different kinds of prestige should be made available to reflect the many different near perfect performances the organization wants to encourage.* Unfortunately, most organizations simply aren't set up to offer many different kinds of prestige. While recognizing the need to empower people, they are still locked into only one kind of prestige—the prestige that comes from having power over someone else. And because they see only one kind of prestige, they have designed only one path toward it: Do well, move up, get more power. Do better, move up higher, get still more power. If a hierarchy is simply a system for apportioning different kinds of prestige to different people, then the flaw of organizations like these is not that they have too much hierarchy but that they have too little. They suffer from a shortage of prestige.

The strengths-based organization must avoid this flaw. It must make different kinds of meaningful prestige widely available. In execution this proves to be a complex, detailed endeavor, but in principle we suggest that there are two basic steps you need to take. First, *your organization must build more ladders.* To do this take each key role and define three basic rungs on the ladder: good, great, and superb. You probably won't use these terms, but no matter what your labels, the highest rung should represent the pinnacle of performance in the role. Also make sure that you identify specific performance criteria (and not just tenure) that must be achieved if the employee is to progress from one rung to the next. Use the balanced scorecard we described earlier to determine the levels of performance required for each rung. The number of rungs and the required performance levels will obviously vary by role, but in the end the purpose of this effort is to be able to say to a new employee in any role, "This is the Tiger Woods level of performance in your role, and this is exactly what you have to achieve in order to reach it."

To which the employee might counter, "Okay, but if I reach this Tiger Woods level of performance, will I be respected in the organization?" The answer had better be yes, or the employee won't bother climbing. So the second step in building a strengths-based career development system is to *give people incentives to climb the rungs.* Obviously the best way to do this is to reallocate prestige so that the higher you climb, the more prestige you get. This means changing your title structure. Why can't your very best store manager, nurse supervisor, salesperson, or even customer service representative have a senior level title? This may sound odd at first, but why shouldn't they warrant a title that carries this level of prestige? If your objective scorecard reveals that they are consistently brilliant at producing the outcomes your organization needs, why withhold prestige simply because they don't have position power over other people? Some might say that these titles shouldn't be given to lower-level roles because it goes against industry norms. This is true, but so what? Most industry norms are not strengths-based, and you probably don't want your organization to be constrained by them.

You will also need to change your pay structure to reflect these increases in prestige. As we described in *First, Break All the Rules,* the most effective way to do this is through broadbanding. This means creating broad bands of pay whereby the employee on the highest rung on the role ladder can earn 30, 40, or even 50 percent more than the employee just beginning his climb.

If you are worried that this will drive up your labor costs, keep in mind that your bands can overlap. If you decide that conceptually there is nothing wrong with a brilliant and experienced customer service representative earning more than a novice manager, then practically you can raise the reps' pay and not raise the managers' pay. Your pay increases won't cascade up the hierarchy.

In addition, by offering incentives to some of your employees to become near perfect performers in their role—the world's best, if you will—you may end up with fewer people doing more and being paid more. Thus, even though some employees will be earning more, your net head count will go down, and so will your labor costs.

You can also decide to designate some of this broad band as "at risk" pay rather than base pay. Since roughly 40 percent of employee benefits are calculated on base pay, you will not see your benefits rise dramatically. In fact, by making meaningful prestige available to as many roles as possible, you may actually reduce your benefit costs significantly. In his latest book, *Genome: the Autobiography of a Species in 23 Chapters,* Matt Ridley describes the connection between job status and health: "In a massive, long-term study of 17,000 [British] civil servants, an almost unbelievable conclusion emerged: the status of a person's job was more able to predict their likelihood of a heart attack than obesity, smoking or high blood pressure. Somebody in a low-grade job, such as a janitor, was nearly four times as likely to have a heart attack as a permanent secretary [the highest level civil servant] at the top of the heap. Indeed, even if the permanent secretary was fat, hypertensive or a smoker, he was still less likely to suffer a heart attack at a given age than a thin, non-smoking, low-blood-pressure janitor. Exactly the same result emerged from a similar study of a million employees of the Bell Telephone Company in the 1960's."

This means that the health of your employees is closely linked to how much prestige you accord their role. The more prestige your organization offers, the healthier your employees will be. Less prestige means sicker employees. In Ridley's words: "Your heart is at the mercy of your pay grade." Gallup's own research extends this connection between strengths-based organizations and the health of their employees. In our latest meta-analysis of 198,000 employees in almost eight thousand business units, employees who strongly agreed that they had a chance to do what they do best every day claimed fewer sick days, filed fewer workers' compensation claims, and had fewer accidents while on the job.

All of the above adds weight to your responsibility for building a strengths-based organization. Yes, if you want a more productive organization, play to each person's strengths. Yes, if you want to create higher levels of customer loyalty, play to each person's strengths. Yes, if you want to retain your most talented employees, play to their strengths. But just as important, if you take the safety and health of your employees seriously, play to their strengths and give them the prestige they deserve for doing so.

* * *

Most organizations are a puzzle put together in a darkened room. Each piece is clumsily squeezed into place and then the edges are ground down so that they feel well positioned. But pull up the shades, let a little light into the room, and we can see the truth. Eight out of ten pieces are in the wrong place.

Eight out of ten employees feel they are miscast. Eight out of ten employees never have the chance to reveal the best of themselves. They suffer for it, their organization suffers, and their customers suffer. Their health, their friends, and their family suffer.

It doesn't have to be this way. We can raise the shades higher still. We can spotlight each person's strengths. We can provide him with a manager who is intrigued by these strengths. We can build an organization that asks him to play to these strengths and that honors him when he does. We can show him the best of himself and ask him to keep reaching for more. We can help him live a strong life.

With the knowledge economy gathering pace, global competition increasing, new technologies quickly commoditized, and the workforce aging, the right employees are becoming more precious with each passing year. Those of us who lead great organizations must become more sophisticated and more efficient when it comes to capitalizing on our people. We must find the best fit possible of people's strengths and the roles we are asking them to play at work. Only then will we be as strong as we should be. Only then will we win.

Appendix: A Technical Report on StrengthsFinder

"What research underpins the StrengthsFinder Profile, and what research is planned to refine the instrument?"

By Theodore L. Hayes, Ph.D., Senior Research Director, The Gallup Organization

There are many technical issues that must be considered when evaluating an instrument such as StrengthsFinder. One set of issues revolves around information technology and the expanding possibilities that Web-based applications offer for those who study human nature. Another set of issues involves what is known as psychometrics, which is the scientific study of human behavior through measurement. There are many American and international standards for psychometrics applied to test development that StrengthsFinder is required to meet (such as AERA/APA/NCME, 1999). The present report deals with some questions that emerge from those standards as well as technical questions that a leader may have about StrengthsFinder's use in his or her organization.

A few technical references have been cited for readers who wish to review primary source material. These technical materials may be found in local university libraries or on the Internet. The reader is encouraged to contact Gallup for further discussion or review the sources cited at the end of the report.

What is StrengthsFinder?
StrengthsFinder is a Web-based assessment of normal personality from the perspective of positive psychology. It is the first assessment

instrument developed expressly for the Internet. There are 180 items in StrengthsFinder, presented to the user over a secure connection. Each item lists a pair of potential self-descriptors, such as "I read instructions carefully" and "I like to jump right into things." The descriptors are placed as if anchoring polar ends of a continuum. The participant is then asked to choose which statement in the pair best describes him or her, and also to what extent that chosen option is descriptive. The participant is given twenty seconds to respond to a given item before the system moves on to the next item. (StrengthsFinder developmental research showed that the twenty-second limit resulted in a negligible item non-completion rate.) The item pairs are grouped into thirty-four themes.

What personality theory is StrengthsFinder based on?

StrengthsFinder is based on a general model of positive psychology. It captures personal motivation (Striving), interpersonal skills (Relating), self-presentation (Impacting), and learning style (Thinking).

What is positive psychology?

Positive psychology is a framework, or a paradigm, that encompasses an approach to psychology from the perspective of healthy, successful life functioning. Topics include optimism, positive emotions, spirituality, happiness, satisfaction, personal development, and well-being. These topics (and similar ones) may be studied at the individual level or in a work group, family, or community. While some who study positive psychology are therapists, a more typical distinction is that therapists focus on *removing* dysfunction, while positive psychologists focus on *maintaining or enhancing* successful function. A recent special issue of the journal *American Psychologist* (2000) gave an over-view of positive psychology by some of its most distinguished academic researchers.

Is StrengthsFinder supposed to be a work-related inventory, a clinical inventory, both, or neither?

StrengthsFinder is an omnibus assessment based on positive psychology. Its main application has been in the work domain, but it has been used for understanding individuals in a variety of settings—families, executive teams, and personal development. It is *not* intended for clinical assessment or diagnosis of psychiatric disorders.

Why isn't StrengthsFinder based on the "big five" factors of personality that have been well established in research journals for over twenty years?

The "big five" factors of personality are neuroticism (which reflects emotional stability), extroversion (seeking the company of others), openness (interest in new experiences, ideas, and so forth), agreeableness (likability, harmoniousness), and conscientiousness (rule abidance, discipline, integrity). A substantial amount of scientific research has demonstrated that human personality functioning can be summarized in terms of these five dimensions. This research has been conducted across cultures and languages (for example, McCrae and Costa, 1987; McCrae, Costa, Lima, et al., 1999; McCrae, Costa, Ostendorf, et al., 2000).

The major reason that StrengthsFinder is not based on the big five is that the big five is a measurement model rather than a conceptual one. It was derived from factor analysis. No theory underpinned it. It consists of the most generally agreed upon minimal number of personality factors, but conceptually it is no more correct than a model with four or six factors (Block, 1995; Hogan, Hogan, and Roberts, 1996). StrengthsFinder could be boiled down to the big five but nothing would be gained from doing so. In fact, reducing the respondent's StrengthsFinder score to five dimensions would produce less information than is produced by any current measure of the big five since those measures also report subscores in addition to the five major dimensions.

Why does StrengthsFinder use these 180 item pairs and not others?

These pairs reflect Gallup's research over three decades of studying successful people in a systematic, structured manner. They were derived from a quantitative review of item functioning, from a content review of the representativeness of themes and items within themes, with an eye toward the construct validity of the entire assessment. Given the breadth of human performance we wish to assess, the pool of items is large and diverse. Well-known personality assessments range from 150 to upward of 400 items.

Are the StrengthsFinder items ipsatively scored, and if so, does this limit scoring of the items?

Ipsativity is a mathematical term that refers to an aspect of a data matrix, such as a set of scores. A data matrix is said to be ipsative when the sum of the scores for each respondent is a constant. More generally, ipsativity refers to a set of scores that define a person in particular but is comparable between persons only in a very limited way. For example, if you rank-ordered your favorite colors and someone else rank-ordered their favorite colors, one could not compare the *intensity* of preference for any particular color due to ipsativity; only the *ranking* could be compared. Out of 180 StrengthsFinder items, less than 30 percent are ipsatively scored. These items are distributed over the range of StrengthsFinder themes, and no one theme contains more than one item scored in a way that would produce an ipsative data matrix (Plake, 1999).

How are theme scores calculated on StrengthsFinder?
Scores are calculated based on the mean of the intensity of self-description. The respondent is given three response options for each self-description: strongly agree, agree, and neutral. A proprietary formula assigns a value to each response category. Values for items in the theme are averaged to derive a theme score. Scores can be reported as a mean, as a standard score, or as a percentile.

Was modern test score theory (for example, IRT) used to develop StrengthsFinder?
StrengthsFinder was developed to capitalize on the accumulated knowledge and experience of Gallup's talent-based strengths practice. Thus, initially items were chosen based on traditional validity evidence (construct, content, criterion). This is a universally accepted method for developing assessments. Methods to apply IRT to assessments that are both heterogeneous and homogeneous are only now being explored (for example, Waller, Thompson, and Wenk, 2000). Further iterations of StrengthsFinder may well use IRT methods to refine the instrument.

What construct validity work links StrengthsFinder to measures of normal personality, abnormal personality, vocational interest, and intelligence?
StrengthsFinder is an omnibus assessment of interpersonal talents based on positive psychology. Therefore, it will undoubtedly have

correlational linkages to these measures to about the same extent that personality measures link to other measures in general. Ultimately, this is an empirical question to be explored in future research.

Can StrengthsFinder scores change?

This is an important question for which there are both technical and conceptual answers.

Technical answers: The talents measured by StrengthsFinder are expected to demonstrate a property called reliability. Reliability has several definitions. One definition of reliability, technically known as internal consistency, is the proportion of the score that is due to the aspects of the theme itself and not to irrelevant influences such as mood, fatigue, and so forth. High internal consistency shows that a theme's items provide a consistent read with each other and do not reflect other influences. Gallup researchers recently investigated the internal reliability of StrengthsFinder themes using data from more than fifty thousand respondents. Because the number of items per StrengthsFinder theme vary—there are between four and fifteen items per theme—the average inter-item correlation for each theme was adjusted to reflect the internal consistency for a fifteen-item theme. This analysis showed that the average internal consistency was .785. The maximum possible internal consistency is 1, and a rule of thumb target for reliability is .80. Thus, StrengthsFinder themes show acceptable internal consistency.

A second definition of reliability, technically known as test-retest, is the extent to which scores are stable over time. Almost all StrengthsFinder themes have a test-retest reliability over a six-month interval between .60 and .80; a maximum test-retest reliability score of 1 would indicate that all StrengthsFinder respondents received *exactly* the same score over two assessments.

Conceptual answers: While an evaluation of the full extent of this stability is, of course, an empirical question, the conceptual origins of a person's talents are also relevant. Gallup has studied the life themes of high performers in a large series of research studies combining qualitative and quantitative investigations over many years. Participants have included youths in their early teens to adults in their mid-seventies. In each of these studies the focal point was the identification of long-standing patterns of thought, feeling, and behavior associated with success. The lines of interview questioning used were both prospective and retrospective, such as "What do you want to be doing ten years from now?" and "At what age did you make your first sale?" In other words, the time frame of interest in our original studies of excellence in job performance was long term, not short term. Many of the items developed provided useful predictions of job stability, thereby suggesting that the measured attributes were of a persistent nature. Tracking studies of job performance over two- to three-year time spans added to the Gallup understanding of what it takes for a job incumbent to be consistently effective, rather than just achieving impressive short-term gains. The prominence of dimensions and items relating to motivation and to values in much of the original life themes research also informed the design of a StrengthsFinder instrument that can identify those enduring human qualities.

At this early stage in the application of StrengthsFinder, it is not yet clear how long an individual's salient features, so measured, will endure. In general, however, it is likely to be years rather than months. We may perhaps project a minimum of five years and upper ranges of thirty to forty years and longer. There is growing evidence (for example, Judge, Higgins, Thoresen, and Barrick, 1999) that some aspects of personality are predictive throughout many decades of the life span. Some StrengthsFinder themes may turn out to be more enduring than others. Cross-sectional studies of different age groups will provide the earliest insights into possible age-related changes in normative patterns of behaviors. The first explanations for apparent changes in themes, as measured, should therefore be sought in the direction of measurement error rather than as indications of a true change in the underlying trait, emotion, or cognition. The respondents themselves should also be invited to offer an explanation for any apparent discrepancies.

Do StrengthsFinder theme scores vary according to race, sex, or age?

Gallup has studied StrengthsFinder themes in the general population. These studies aim to reflect all possible respondents in general, not applicants for or incumbents in a particular position. Score differences between major demographic groups tend to average under .04 points (i.e., four hundredths of a point) at this worldwide theme database level.

Practically speaking, these score differences are trivial. There is also no consistent pattern to the score differences. For example, one of the most important sales-related themes might be Achiever. For Achiever, males score higher than females by .031 points; nonwhite (minority group) individuals score higher than white (majority group) individuals by .048 points; and people under forty years of age score higher than those forty and over by .033 points. An important theme for managers might be Arranger. For this theme females score higher than males by .021 points; white (majority group) individuals score higher than nonwhite (minority group) individuals by .016 points; and people under forty years of age score lower than those forty and over by .053 points. Finally, many people believe that Empathy is an important theme for teaching, in particular, and human relations, in general. For this theme females score higher than males by .248 points; white (majority group) individuals score higher than nonwhite (minority group) individuals by .030 points; and people under forty score higher than those forty and over by .014 points.

Statistically speaking, with more than fifty thousand respondents in the current StrengthsFinder database, even some of these very small score differences may be deemed "statistically significant." This is simply a function of sample size. It is critical to note that the average effect size difference, expressed in units referred to as "d-prime," between men and women over all themes is .099 (that is, the average correlation between theme difference and group membership is under .05); the average d-prime effect size difference between whites and nonwhites is .133 (the average correlation equivalent is under .07); and the average d-prime effect size difference between those under forty years of age and those at least forty is .050 (the average correlation equivalent is under .03). Also, many of these small differences are favorable for what one might consider "protected" groups—nonwhites, women, and those forty or more. Finally, even significant differences do not indicate that one group has a "better" theme score than another, only that at the database level we might expect to see trends in scores for particular groups.

In reviewing these results, four conclusions seem clear to Gallup researchers. First, the average differences between theme scores for protected versus majority groups are very small, typically under .04 points, which translates to a d-prime difference score under .10. Thus, there is no obvious or measurement-level bias in score distributions between these groups. There is 98–100 percent overlap between score distributions for comparable groups.

Second, score differences are extremely small and are only statistically significant in a few cases. This is due to the fact that more than fifty thousand respondents have completed StrengthsFinder, thus over-magnifying almost any score difference. Even when there are significant differences, the protected group is typically favored.

Third, no one theme is better than another. They simply represent the potential for different kinds of strengths. Strength building is not a zero-sum game.

In summary, trivially small differences at the worldwide database level do not translate into important practical differences at the individual level.

How can StrengthsFinder be administered, scored, and reported for individuals who are unable to use the Internet either because of disability or economic status?

In regard to economic status (a.k.a. the digital divide), possible solutions include accessing the Internet from a library or school. It should be noted that some organizations that Gallup works with do not have universal Internet access. In these cases, as with those from disadvantaged backgrounds, the solution generally has involved special access from a few central locations.

In regard to disability, a range of accommodations is available. Generally, the most effective is for the participant to turn off the timer that governs the pace of StrengthsFinder administration. Beyond this, accommodations would need to be arranged with Gallup on a case-by-case basis in advance of taking StrengthsFinder.

What is the reading level for StrengthsFinder? What alternatives are available for those who do not meet that level?

StrengthsFinder is designed for completion by those with at least an eighth- to tenth-grade reading level (that is, by most fourteen-year-olds). Trials of StrengthsFinder in our youth leadership studies have demonstrated neither significant nor consistent problems in completion of StrengthsFinder among teens. Possible alternatives or accommodations include turning off the timer feature to allow for checking a dictionary or to ask about the meaning of a word.

Is StrengthsFinder appropriate for non-English speakers?

There is overwhelming evidence from both Gallup and other research organizations that personality dimensions such as those measured by StrengthsFinder are the same across cultures. What changes is the level of the score, not the nature of the theme. StrengthsFinder is currently available in fourteen languages.

What feedback does a candidate get from StrengthsFinder?

Feedback varies depending on the reason the person completes the StrengthsFinder Profile. Sometimes the respondent receives only a report listing his or her top five themes—those where the person scored the highest. In other situations the person may also review the remaining thirty-one themes, along with action suggestions for each theme, in a personal feedback session with a Gallup consultant or in a supervised team-building session with their colleagues.

References

The following references are provided for those readers interested in particular details of this technical report. This reference list is not meant to be exhaustive, and although many use advanced statistical techniques, the reader should not be deterred from reviewing them.

American Educational Research Association, American Psychological Association, National Council on Measurement in Education (AERA/APA/NCME). 1999. *Standards for educational and psychological testing.* Washington, D.C.: American Educational Research Association.

American Psychologist. Positive psychology [special issue]. 2000. Washington, D.C.: American Psychological Association.

Block, J. 1995. A contrarian view of the five-factor approach to personality description. *Psychological Bulletin* 117:187–215.

Hogan, R., J. Hogan, and B. W. Roberts. 1996. Personality measurement and employment decisions: Questions and answers. *American Psychologist* 51:469–77.

Hunter, J. E., and F. L. Schmidt. 1990. *Methods of meta-analysis: Correcting error and bias in research findings.* Newbury Park, CA: Sage.

Judge, T. A., C. A. Higgins, C. J. Thoresen, and M. R. Barrick. 1999. The big five personality traits, general mental ability, and career success across the life span. *Personnel Psychology* 52:621–52.

Lipsey, M. W., and D. B. Wilson. 1993. The efficacy of psychological, educational, and behavioral treatment. *American Psychologist* 48:1181–1209.

McCrae, R. R., and P. T. Costa. 1987. Validation of the five-factor model of personality across instruments and observers. *Journal of Personality and Social Psychology* 52:81–90.

McCrae, R. R., P. T. Costa, M. P. de Lima, et al. 1999. Age differences in personality across the adult life span: Parallels in five cultures. *Developmental Psychology* 35:466–77.

McCrae, R. R., P. T. Costa, F. Ostendorf, et al. 2000. Nature over nurture: Temperament, personality, and life span development. *Journal of Personality and Social Psychology* 78:173–86.

Plake, B. 1999. *An investigation of ipsativity and multicollinearity properties of the StrengthsFinder Instrument* [technical report]. Lincoln, NE: The Gallup Organization.

Waller, N. G., J. S. Thompson, and E. Wenk. 2000. Using IRT to separate measurement bias from true group differences on homogeneous *and* heterogeneous scales: An illustration with the MMPI. *Psychological Methods* 5:125–46.

Acknowledgments

This book is the product of many years of research into talents and strengths. We must thank the many Gallup associates around the world whose insights fueled the research and ultimately led to the discoveries presented here.

In particular, we acknowledge Jim Clifton and Larry Emond who focused the book; Drs. Connie Rath and James Sorensen who have lived out their belief in talent; the research expertise of Drs. Gale Muller, Dennison Bhola, and Ted Hayes, which grounded the concepts; Dr. Kathie Sorensen, who leads our efforts to help people develop their strengths; Dr. Rosemary Travis, who conducted so many of the strengths interviews quoted in this book; Tom Rath and Jon Conradt, who made the technology underpinning the StrengthsFinder Profile fast, robust, and reliable; Jurita Anschutz, Julie Clement, and Mark Rupprecht, who crafted the Web site; Antoinette Southwick, Sharon Lutz, and Penelope Baker, who built the relationships and made all the arrangements work perfectly; Bette Kurd, who listened so carefully to our interviewees; and Alec Gallup, who may have read through the manuscript more times than the two authors combined.

We also have many to thank outside the Gallup family: Richard Hutton for his storytelling prowess; our friends at William Morris, Joni Evans and Jennifer Sherwood, who continue to guide us through the book world; our editor at Free Press, Fred Hills, and his colleague Veera Hiranandani, for their judgment and their discipline; Mitch and Linda Hart for their strength and support; and, of course, our families.

To help us in our writing we asked hundreds of people to take the StrengthsFinder Profile and then describe their signature themes at work. This was no small investment on their part. Their willingness to make this investment, to tolerate our questions, and to reveal their successes and struggles brought our book to life. Thank you all.

About the Authors

Marcus Buckingham graduated from Cambridge University in 1987 with a master's degree in social and political science. During his seventeen years with The Gallup Organization, Buckingham helped lead research into the world's best leaders, managers and workplaces. He is the co-author of the bestselling *First, Break All the Rules* and his new book, *The One Thing You Need to Know* will be published in the UK in June 2005. Now an independent consultant and speaker, Buckingham is considered one of the world's leading authorities on employee productivity and the practices of leading and managing.

Donald O. Clifton, Ph.D. (1924-2003), was cited by the American Psychological Association as the Father of Strengths Psychology and the Grandfather of Positive Psychology. He was a chairman of Gallup, Inc., and he invented the Clifton StrengthsFinder, an assessment that has helped more than 1 million people around the world discover their talents. He co-authored several books, including the #1 *New York Times* bestseller *How Full Is Your Bucket?*.